Author: Carl W

Copyrigl

About the
(God's Blessin

I was born in this great country on June 19th, 1933, to Charles and Eva (Mallow) Rice. We were just country folks in the commonwealth of Pennsylvania, on a two-hundred and fourty-three acre farm. We farmed the land by horses and Mother and Dad raised eight children there.

During the great depression and through the Great World War II, the Rice family were members of a little country church with about 25 or 40 members, with a circuit minister. Every other Sunday he would come and preach.

In the spring of 1947 an evangelist by the name of Sadie Triplett came and preached a revival. The Lord saved me and in 1948 called me to preach. At the end of March or April, I preached my first message from I Peter 1:18-19 (Forasmuch as ye know that ye were not redeemed with corruptible things, as silver and gold, from your vain conversation received by tradition from your fathers; But with the precious blood of Christ, as of a lamb without blemish and without spot :) I was so scared, I only preached for a few moments. I was so scared I couldn't read my notes.

In the year of 1949, an evangelist by the name of T. J. Bryant came and preached a revival in our church. I was so hungry for the word I talked to Brother Bryant and he pointed me to God's Bible School and College in Cincinnati, Ohio, where I left my folks and the farm for a life of studying the Word of God. Here I was, 17 years old and now studying under some of the greatest professors in my time. After a few months I was teaching evangelistic work in school. I thank God for His wisdom.

I worked my way through school, going to school from 8:00 a.m. until 12:00 noon, then chapel. After noon, at 2:00 p.m. I would take students on the field and train them in evangelistic work in hospitals, jails and street meetings and in the homes. After my schooling was paid for, I made 9 cents an hour over my room and board and books. I was a night watchman and telephone operator. I was blessed so much. My job was made easy by the Lord.

By the year of 1951 I was very blessed by a wonderful girl (Eva Joyce Ross) that I met while training her in jail work. Our first date was in a jail (ha ha), but she was the one God blessed me with. We were married in July of 1952. After we were married God blessed us with six children. As of this date in 2013, we have 61 years of marriage.

It was a blessing to be married to Joyce. She was a Freshman in High School when we met. Thank God. I couldn't have made it this far without her. She is my helpmate and friend. I'm so glad we made it together this far and will until death do us part.

Just thought you might like a little history lesson on my life over the years. Sure, we've made mistakes, but God has helped us through them all. In our marriage and all through life, without Christ we would have never made it. ***Thanks for the lovely years.***

Love & Prayers   Brother Carl

Table of Contents

PROLOGUE

In the study of the Book of John, we want to show the life of Christ as John saw it, from eternity to eternity; to show who <u>He</u> was, who <u>He</u> is and who <u>He</u> will be.

John's book as 21 chapters and we want to study each chapter as John saw Him in 21 different aspects of life. We want to explain why John's Gospel is different from the other three in some manner.

First, in Matthew, Mark, and Luke, Christ's miracles are basically to show His power. In the Gospel of John, John show's Christ's Miracles as a discourse:

1. For example, the thirst at Jacob's Well was followed by the discourse of Living Water in John 4:7-14

   7 There cometh a woman of Samaria to draw water: Jesus saith unto her, give me to drink.

   8 (For his disciples were gone away unto the city to buy meat.)

   9 Then saith the woman of Samaria unto him, how is it that thou, being a Jew, askest drink of me, which am a woman of Samaria? For the Jews have no dealings with the Samaritans.

   10 Jesus answered and said unto her, If thou knewest the gift of God, and who it is that saith to thee, Give me to drink; thou wouldest have asked of him, and he would have given thee living water.

   11 The woman saith unto him, Sir, thou hast nothing to draw with, and the well is deep: from whence then hast thou that living water?

   12 Art thou greater than our father Jacob, which gave us the well, and drank thereof himself, and his children, and his cattle?

   13 Jesus answered and said unto her, whosoever drinketh of this water shall thirst again:

   14 But whosoever drinketh of the water that I shall give him shall never thirst; but the water that I shall give him shall be in him a well of water springing up into everlasting life.

2. The feeding of 5,000 was followed by the discourse of the Bread of Life in John 6:35.

   35 And Jesus said unto them, I am the bread of life: he that cometh to me shall never hunger; and he that believeth on me shall never thirst.

3. In John, the miracles are usually teaching signs as in John 2:11 or signs revealed in John 20:30-31.

   2:11 this beginning of miracles did Jesus in Cana of Galilee, and manifested forth his glory; and his disciples believed on him.

   20:30 and many other signs truly did Jesus in the presence of his disciples, which are not written in this book:

³¹ But these are written, that ye might believe that Jesus is the Christ, the Son of God; and that believing ye might have life through his name.

There are three key words here: (a) Sign (b) Believe (c) Life

The content of the Gospel of John shows the <u>Deity of Christ</u>.

1. Jesus is called God twice: John 1:1 and John 20:28
2. Jesus is called the Only Begotten Son of God ten times: John 1:14, 18, 34 & 49; 3:16 & 18; 6:69; 9:35; 10:36 and 11:27
3. Jesus is equal with God four times: John 5:18; 10:30; 14:9 and 16:27
4. John records His relationship with the Father 116 times as "Your Father", "The Father", or "My Father", but never "Our Father".
5. John records four times that Jesus never sinned: John 8:46; 18:38; 19:4 & 6.
6. The attributes of His deity are used to refer t Jesus as
   a. Omnipresent: John 1:17 & 3:13
   b. Omnipotence: John 5:21; 6:19 & 10:18
   c. Omniscience: John 2:25 & 11:11-14

Jesus uses "I am" many times.

1. I am <u>the Messiah</u>: John 4:25-26
2. I am <u>the Bread of Life</u>: John 6:35, 41, 48 & 51
3. I am <u>the light of the world</u>: John 8:12; 9:5 & 12;46
4. I am <u>the door</u>: John 10:7 & 9
5. I am <u>the Good Shepherd</u>: John 10:11& 14
6. I am <u>the Resurrection and the Life</u>: John 11:25
7. I am <u>the way, the truth and the life</u>: John 14:6
8. I am <u>the true vine</u>.: John 15:1 & 5
9. John records Christ as saying "before Abraham was, <u>I am</u>.: John 8:58
10. And last, the greatest on...I am <u>He</u>.: John 18:5 & Exodus 3:14
11. The Great I Am was there in the beginning, is there now, and will be there in the greatest event of al times: John 1:1-5; Genesis 1:5; Revelation 21:6-7; Revelation 1:8; Revelation 4:8 and Isaiah 4:1-4

NOTES TO READERS:

When reading this book, you will find that each chapter covers a single chapter of John (i.e. Chapter 1 covers John 1). Therefore, when reading throughout the chapter you will find verses that are enclosed in a text box. These verses are found in the corresponding chapter (i.e. if the text box is in Chapter 1, and it says **Verse 11**, this means it is found in John 1:11).

All references to "Strong's Number" are definitions from the Strong's Concordance.

To begin our study on the Book of John, we begin with....

CHAPTER 1
Jesus, the Son of God

The key word here is "word". In the Old Testament, creation was y the spoken word of God. "And God <u>said</u> let there be...

Light (Genesis 1:3-5);
Firmament (Genesis 1:6);
Land and Sea (Genesis 1:9);
Grass & Herbs (Genesis 1:11);
Lights in the Firmament (Genesis 1:14);
Fishes and Birds (Genesis 1:20-22
Animals (Genesis 1:25)

The six days of creation were brought forth by the word: **John 1:3**

Let's look at Genesis 3:15: And I will put enmity between thee and the woman, and between thy seed and her seed; it shall bruise thy head, and thou shalt bruise his heel.

The Adamic covenant was introduced at the beginning of this period.
1. The serpent was cursed: Genesis 1:14
2. God promised redemption through the seed of the woman: Genesis 1:15
3. The woman would experience sorrow and pain in child bearing: Genesis 1:16
4. The earth was cursed: Genesis 1:17-18
5. Sorrow, pain and physical death became an experience of life: Genesis 1:19
6. Man failed under this covenant and people did evil continually: Genesis 6:5
7. God judged them by the flood: Genesis 9:12
8. In the scripture, Genesis 1:15, Christ would deliver the last hard blow to Satan. He would be bruised Himself on the cross but would cause the crushing of Satan and his kingdom.

We look now at the birth of Jesus, or the Son of God, as He became flesh – **John 1:14**

A sign shall be given – Isaiah 7:14; Matthew 1:23; Luke 1:31; Isaiah 9:6

A son was promised and to prove the lineage of Christ we must look at two scriptures to prove more about the Son of God.

1. The Royal Line back to Abraham – Matthew 1:1-17

Now we turn to Jeremiah 22:30. Notice what it says, "Write ye this man childless." This means no descendant of Jehoiakim's seven sons (I Chronicles 3:17-18) would ever succeed him to the throne of Judah, nor would any of his natural descendants succeed him. This line in Matthew 1:11-16 as the line of descent is thus recorded to show Jesus legal right to the throne of David. By tracing Jesus ancestry through to King David through the line of Davidic kings, Matthew connects Jesus with the royal lineage or heritage.

The genealogy shows that Joseph, Jesus' legal earthly father, traces his blood lines back to Abraham. This also was a fulfillment of the covenant promise to Abraham the forefather of the Jews. (Genesis 12:3; 13:15 & 22:18). This was emphasizing Jesus' Jewish parents.

Notice that very carefully Matthew avoids giving an impression that Joseph was the natural father of Jesus, but only as Mary's husband. (Matthew 1:19)

2. Now let's look at Jesus lineage back to Adam – Luke 3:23-38

Now we must not lose sight of the virgin birth. We know that the blood line come from the <u>father</u>, but notice John 1:14 – "The Word was made <u>flesh</u>." Now turn your minds to Leviticus 17:11 – "The life of the flesh is in the blood." Notice Mary's saying in Luke 1:34-35 – "Then said Mary unto the angel, how shall this be, seeing I know not a man?" And the angel answered and said unto her, The <u>Holy Ghost</u> shall come upon thee, and the power of the Highest (*or Most High*) shall overshadow thee: therefore, also that holy thing (*or Holy One*) which shall be born of thee shall be called the Son of God."

The Genealogy of Jesus

LUKE 3
Verse 23[a]
And Jesus himself began (*or began his ministry*) to be about thirty years of age, being (as was supposed) the son of Joseph.

We take Luke's Chapter 3 and see the legal line back to Adam. These 15 verses carry the lineage back to where it all started…at Adam.

Verse 38 [b]
…which was the son of Adam, which was the son of God.

Now let's notice in…

JOHN 1
VERSE 1 [a]
John now takes us back to the beginning, before Adam was formed from the dust of the earth. "In the beginning was the Word (*or Jesus*), and the Word was with God, and the Word was God."
Now we see the <u>Deity</u> of Christ from eternity past to eternity future.

REVELATION 21
Verse 6 [a]
And he said unto me, it is done. I am <u>Alpha</u> and Omega, the beginning and the end.

We now have Him from before Adam and He will be in the future. His deity is from everlasting to everlasting.

The word "everlasting" means eternal, lasting through all time".

Let's look at his Kingly lineage.

MATTHEW 1
Verse 1
The book of the generation of Jesus Christ, the son of David, the son of Abraham.

The first 16 verses of Matthew 1 will show His lineage to the throne of David

Verse 16
And Jacob begat Joseph the husband of Mary, of whom was born Jesus, who is called Christ.

Om the Gospel of Luke we see His legal lineage going back to God himself, and in Matthew we have His kingly lineage going back to Abraham. Here, we can see that Luke does not lose sight of the Virgin Birth, for he said in Lune 3:23 "**as was supposed** the son of Joseph". Luke demonstrates that Christ's ancestry shows both through David and Abraham. Even more, he traces the lineage back to Adam and then back to God. He makes two points.

1. Jesus had an ancient place in the race of mankind.
2. He was God's anointed deliverer.

Jesus has significance for all of humanity and not just for the people of Israel.

ACTS 2
Verse 29
Men and brethren, let me freely speak unto you of the patriarch <u>David</u> that he is both dead and buried, and his sepulcher is with us unto this day.

Verse 30
Therefore, being a prophet, and knowing that God had sworn with an oath to him, that of the fruit of his loins, according to the flesh, he would raise up Christ to sit on his throne;

ISAIAH 9
Verse 6
For unto us a child is born, unto us a son is given: and the government shall be upon his shoulder: and his name shall be called <u>Wonderful</u>, Counsellor, the mighty God, The everlasting Father, The Prince of Peace.

Notice....

1. Wonderful – meaning "unusually good, admirable, astonishing, marvelous
2. Counselor – meaning "an advisor"
3. Mighty God – meaning "all powerful God"
4. Everlasting Father – meaning "eternal, lasting through all time"
5. Prince of Peace – meaning "a Ruler"

WONDERFUL

PSALMS 78
Verse 4
We will not hide them from their children, shewing to the generation to come the praises of the LORD, and his strength, and his <u>wonderful</u> works that he hath done.

COUNSELOR

PSALMS 15
Verse 22
Without counsel purposes are disappointed (*or plans go away*): but in the multitude of counsellors they are established.

THE MIGHTY GOD

I CHRONICLES 29
Verse 13
Both riches and honour came of thee, and thou reignest over all; and in thine hand is power and might; and in thine hand it is to make great, and to give strength unto all.

EVERLASTING FATHER

PSALMS 139
Verse 23
Search me, O God, and know my heart: try me, and know my thoughts:

Verse 24
And see if there be any wicked way in me, and lead me in the way everlasting.

PRINCE OF PEACE

ACTS 5
Verse 31
Him hath God exalted with his right hand to be a Prince and a Saviour, for to give repentance to Israel, and forgiveness of sins.

ISAIAH 11
Verse 2
And the spirit of the LORD shall rest upon him, the spirit of <u>wisdom</u> and <u>understanding</u>, the spirit of <u>counsel</u> and <u>might</u>, the spirit of <u>knowledge</u> and of the fear of the LORD;

In these scriptures, the time of the Messiah's coming was undoubtedly a puzzle to Old Testament times. In verse 1 (Isaiah 11:1) the Prophet indicates His coming in the distant future. Isaiah here predicts that the tree or the line of David, will be cut down and that a shoot must then grow out of the stalk (*or root*) of Jesse before it will flourish again. He predicts that a rod will come forth from the stem of Jesse (David's father).

The "spirit of the Lord" refers to the sevenfold spirits of God.

REVELATION 4
Verse 5
And out of the throne proceeded lightnings and thunderings and voices: and there were seven lamps of fire burning before the throne, which are the seven Spirits of God.

ZECHARIAH 3
Verse 9
For behold the *stone* that I have laid before Joshua; upon <u>one</u> stone shall be <u>seven eyes</u>: behold, I will engrave the graving (*or inscription*) thereof, saith the LORD of hosts, and I will remove the iniquity of that land in one day.

The Stone

The stone is used frequently throughout the Old Testament to refer to the Messiah.

- Genesis 49:24 >>>>> Matthew 21:42
- Psalms 118:22 >>>>> Acts 4:11
- Isaiah 28:16 >>>>>>> I Peter 2:6

Now let's see what seven spirits or the seven eyes are.

Isaiah 11
Verse 2

1. The Spirit of the Lord
2. The Spirit of Wisdom
3. The Spirit of Counsel
4. The Spirit of Might
5. The Spirit of Knowledge
6. The Spirit of the Fear of the Lord

The number seven denotes the perfection of the Spirit. It is God's perfect number. It denotes the perfection and completion, totality and universality.

CHAPTER 2
JESUS, THE SON OF MAN

JOHN 2
Verse 1
And the third day there was a marriage in Cana of Galilee; and the mother of Jesus was there:

Verse 2
And both Jesus was called (or invite), and his disciples, to the marriage.

Verse 3
And when they wanted wine (or ran out of wine), the mother of Jesus saith unto him, they have no wine.

Verse 4
Jesus saith unto her, Woman, what have I (or what does your concern have to do with me) to do with thee? mine hour is not yet come.

Verse 5
His mother saith unto the servants, whatsoever he saith unto you, do it.

Verse 6
And there were set there six waterpots of stone, after (or according to) the manner of the purifying of the Jews, containing two or three firkins apiece.

Verse 7
Jesus saith unto them, Fill the waterpots with water. And they filled them up to the brim.

Verse 8
And he saith unto them, Draw out now (or draw some out now), and bear (or take it to) unto the governor of the feast. And they bare it.

Verse 9
When the ruler (or master) of the feast had tasted the water that was made wine, and knew not whence it was: (but the servants which drew the water knew ;) the governor of the feast called the bridegroom,

Verse 10
And saith unto him, every man at the beginning doth set forth good wine; and when men have well drunk, then that which is worse: but thou hast kept the good wine until now.

Verse 11
This beginning of miracles did Jesus in Cana of Galilee, and manifested (or revealed) forth his glory; and his disciples believed on him.

Notice in the last verse of Chapter 1

We see a special advent being fulfilled. We see angels ascending and descending upon the Son of Man. In this passage, perhaps it was because of the prayers sent Heavenward and then answered. Jesus is presented as the stairs between Heaven and Earth. Remember Jacob's ladder?

GENESIS 28
Verse 10
And Jacob went out from Beersheba, and went toward Haran.

Verse 11
And he lighted upon (*or came to*) a certain place, and tarried (*or stayed*) there all night, because the sun was set; and he took of the stones of that place, and put them for his pillows (*or put a stone at his head*), and lay down in that place to sleep.

Verse 12
And he dreamed, and behold a ladder set up on the earth, and the top of it reached to heaven: and behold the angels of God ascending and descending on it.

Here we see the streams of angels ascending and descending, which indicates the appropriateness of this rendering. Jesus took this figure of means of access between Heaven and Earth as a picture of himself.

When Stephen spoke of Him...

ACTS 7
Verse 57
And said, Behold, I see the heavens opened, and the Son of man standing on the right hand of God.

...he referred to the Messiah, as Messiah Jesus fulfilled the three anointed offices.

1. Prophet = He is our spokesman to God.
2. Priest = He is our representative before God.
3. King = He is the ruler of lives in God's subjects.

JESUS, THE DIVIE TEACHER

JOHN 3
Verse 1
There was a man of the Pharisees, named Nicodemus, a ruler of the Jews:

Verse 2
The same came to Jesus by night, and said unto him, Rabbi, we know that thou art a teacher come from God: for no man can do these miracles (or signs) that thou doest, except God be with him.

Verse 3
Jesus answered and said unto him, verily, verily, I say unto thee, except a man be born again (or from above), he cannot see the kingdom of God.

Verse 4
Nicodemus saith unto him, how can a man be born when he is old? Can he enter the second time into his mother's womb, and be born?

Verse 5
Jesus answered, Verily, verily, I say unto thee, except a man be born of water and of the Spirit, he cannot enter into the kingdom of God.

Verse 6
That which is born of the flesh is flesh; and that which is born of the Spirit is spirit.

Here Jesus was talking to a Jewish Pharisee, a ruler of the Jews, a member of the Sanhedrin and a <u>master of Israel</u>. In Verse 5 Jesus states, "Verily, verily (or amen, amen)." The next few words mean so much to us today...

BORN AGAIN

The scriptures states, "except a man be born again" (means "from above"). So, Jesus made a perfect statement, "a man must be born of water and of the Spirit."

I CORINTHIANS 15
Verse 44
It is sown a natural body; it is raised a spiritual body. <u>There is a natural body, and there is a spiritual body.</u>

Verse 45
And so it is written, the first man Adam was made a living soul; the last Adam was made a quickening (*or a life giving*) spirit.

Verse 46
Howbeit that was not first which is spiritual, but that which is natural; and afterward that which is spiritual.

Verse 47
The first man is of the earth, earthy (*or a man made from dust*); the second man is the Lord from heaven.

Verse 48
As is the earthy (*or a man made from dust*), such are they also that are earthy: and as is the heavenly, such are they also that are heavenly.

Verse 49
And as we have borne the <u>image</u> of the earthy (*or a man made from dust*), we shall also bear the image of the heavenly.

Let's look at Romans 5:14 –

ROMANS 5
Verse 13
For until the law sin was in the world: but sin is not imputed when there is no law.
Verse 14
Nevertheless, death reigned from Adam to Moses, even over them that had not sinned after the similitude (*or likeness*) of Adam's transgression, who is the figure (*or a type*) of him that was to come.

"Sin was in this world" gives evidence to the universal presence of sin. The point of these verses (13-14) is that since there was not law between Adam and Moses by which men could be held accountable, the very fact that they all died indicates that God was holding them responsible for the transgression of Adam. This is not unjust, for the principle also works in reverse. Sinners can be called righteous and hence live through Christ.

Here Paul sets forth three contrasts:

1. The first one shows that if Adam's sin caused man to die, the gift by the Grace of Christ also abounds to man.
2. The second one indicates that Adam brings about judgment and condemnation while Christ brings justification (or just-if-I'd-never-sinned).
3. The third one is that Adam's transgression brings in the reign of death, while Christ's righteous obedience results in a reign of life.

We are not saying all will be saved. Adam's sin affects all mankind, while Christ's righteousness is for those who are born again and live for Him as a part of His spiritual race. As Adam was the head of all the human race, we were all in his loins or from the seed of Adam. So, we were all in the body of Adam when he sinned. When Adam sinned, we were actually sinning with him. So, in a sense, every member of the <u>Human Race</u> played a part in Adam's fall.

So, Adam's vote to sin is like the Congressman or Senator who votes to accept the indebtedness in our land makes every American accountable for that indebtedness. Adam's vote to sin made all of mankind indebted to sin. But while Adam's disobedience resulted in the human race being plunged into sin, the obedience of Christ (the second Adam) gives Christians the power to overcome sin in their lives (the sin indebtedness).

ROMANS 8
Verse 29
For whom he did foreknow, he also did predestinate to be conformed to the image of his Son, that he might be the firstborn among many brethren.

The word "foreknow" is not simple prescience or advance knowledge. This knowledge also should not be understood in the sense of being acquainted with, as Adam was acquainted with Eve prior to Genesis 4:1. Until this verse, he only was acquainted with her, but here in Verse 1 it shows of the acquaintance becoming a special relationship as Adam "knew" Eve. Foreknowledge is Gods determination from Eternity to bring man in to a special relationship with himself.

EPHESIANS 1
Verse 5
Having predestinated us unto the adoption of children *(or as sons)* by Jesus Christ to himself, according to the good pleasure of his will,

The goal of predestination is not to send certain ones to Hell and some to Heaven, but is the believer's glorification to make every Christian more like His son. When Abraham was without a son he considered adopting Eliezer as his heir to his household. Because the born-again Christian is an adopted son of God, he can enjoy an intimacy with his Heavenly Father.

GALATIANS 4
Verse 6
And because ye are sons, God hath sent forth the Spirit of his Son into your hearts, crying, Abba, Father.

Verse 7
Wherefore thou art no more a servant, but a son; and if a son, then an heir of God through Christ.

Here in these verses every child of God is given the Spirit the moment he is adopted by God the Father through His Son Jesus Christ. The Spirit gives us the awareness that God is our father.

Paul now instructs the believer that he is no longer under the law. He, instead, is a son, that is a full-grown adult son, who does not need the law's instruction and guidance.

Now let's go back to the verse in John concerning being "born of the water and of the spirit." We have seen that we bore the image of the natural (or the man made of dust) and what disobedience brought in man. We see a man must be born of water or a natural birth of a woman, and now we must have a birth by the Spirit. Born of water implies natural or physical birth and born of the spirit indicates supernatural spiritual birth. These verses of the New Birth implies:

1. It indicates Jewish dependence on being sons of Abraham (John 8:39).
2. It reveals that there must be a work of God from above since the Jews consider children a blessing from God.
3. It teaches the necessity of a new beginning.

Verse 16
For God so loved the world, that he gave his only begotten Son, that whosoever believeth in him should not perish, but have everlasting life.

Verse 17
For God sent not his Son into the world to condemn the world; but that the world through him might be saved.

Notice, love is both an attitude of God and a description of His being. He alone is the divine love and the source of all true love. His love is unconditional and consistently seeks the highest good of the one whom is loved. God's love was clearly demonstrated at Calvary when Jesus died for our sins.

I JOHN 3
Verse 1
Behold, what manner of love the Father hath bestowed upon us, that we should be called the sons of God: therefore, the world knoweth us not, because it knew him not.

"Bestowed" here in this scripture is suggesting the enduring effect of this love that God has given. Believers are children related to God by Christ Jesus or God's amazing love.

I JOHN 3
Verse 2
Beloved, now are we the sons (*or children*) of God, and it doth not yet appear what we shall be: but we know that, when he shall appear, we shall be like him; for we shall see him as he is.

I JOHN 2
Verse 28
And now, little children, abide in him; that, when he shall appear, we may have confidence, and not be ashamed before him at his coming.

At Jesus' coming we shall be transformed into His likeness.

2 CORINTHIANS 3
Verse 18
But we all, with open face (*or unveiled*) beholding as in a glass (*or mirror*) the glory of the Lord, are changed (*or being transformed*) into the same image from glory to glory, even as by the Spirit of the Lord.

The term "beholding as in a glass" has the sense of reflecting. The believer reflects the glory of his Lord, just as Moses reflected the Glory of God. But Moses' glory eventually faded away. <u>But</u> under the New Covenant, the believer is changed into the same image. This transformation takes place by the abiding presence of The Spirit of God.

2 CORINTHIANS 3
Verse 6
Who also hath made us able (*or sufficient*) ministers of the New Testament (*or new covenant*); not of the letter (*or law*), but of the spirit: for the letter (*or law*) killeth, but the spirit giveth life.

Let's look at another verse...

2 CORINTHIANS 3
Verse 3
Forasmuch as ye are manifestly declared to be the epistle of Christ ministered by us, written not with ink, but with the Spirit of the living God; not in tables of stone (*or the ten commandments*), but in fleshy tables of the heart.

EXODUS 32
Verse 16
And the tables were the work of God, and the writing was the writing of God, graven upon the tables.

PROVERBS 3
Verse 3
Let not mercy (*or loving kindness*) and truth forsake thee: bind them about thy neck; write them upon the table of thine heart:

Verse 5
Trust in the LORD with all thine heart; and lean not unto thine own understanding.

Verse 6
In all thy ways acknowledge him, and he shall direct (*or make smooth and straight*) thy paths.

Notice, three commands are given here in these verses:

1. trust: meaning to rely on or depend on
2. lean not: meaning do not depend on your own instincts
3. acknowledge Him: meaning have fellowship and intimacy with God in all of life

Thus, the results of such devotions is God will make your path straight before you.

JOHN 4
Verse 7
There cometh a woman of Samaria to draw water: Jesus saith unto her, give me to drink.

Note

Here that Jesus is addressing the woman one of seven times in this chapter and gradually leading up to
<u>I am He, the Messiah.</u>

At the well, young men who wished to marry would go to the well where young women would come and draw water. It was also a place where two worlds met, sin and righteousness.

1. Give me drink
2. If you would ask, I will give you living water
3. I will give you a well of water of eternal life
4. Go call thy husband
5. You have had five husbands and the one you have now is not your husband
6. Worship God in spirit and truth
7. I am He

Verse 9
Then saith the woman of Samaria unto him, how is it that thou, being a Jew, askest drink of me, which am a woman of Samaria? For the Jews have no dealings with the Samaritans.

Verse 10
Jesus answered and said unto her, If thou knewest the gift of God, and who it is that saith to thee, Give me to drink; thou wouldest have asked of him, and he would have given thee living water.

There are ten gifts listed here in John's gospel that were available for this woman.

1. Grace and truth (John 1:17)
2. Living water (John 4:10)
3. Holy Spirit (John 7:37-39)
4. Perfect example (John 13:15)
5. God's word (John 17:8 & 13:15)
6. The Glory of God (John 17:22)
7. The True Bread (John 6:32)

8. Eternal life (John 6:33 & 10:27-29)
9. Peace (John 14:27)
10. answer to prayer (John 15:16 & 16:23)

The last words of this verse are so precious to a sinner who does not have any hope without Christ, "He would have given thee living water" (unfailing and eternal water).

JEREMIAH 2
Verse 13

For my people have committed two evils; they have forsaken me the <u>fountain</u> of living waters, and hewed them out cisterns, broken cisterns, that can hold no water.

Only God alone can bring fresh living water necessary for a thirsty soul. Israel had left the purity of living waters for polluted cistern, contaminated and broken cisterns that held no water.

ZECHARIAH13
Verse 1

In that day there shall be a fountain opened to the house of David and to the inhabitants of Jerusalem for sin and for uncleanness.

Here "the fountain" refers to the Jews finally accepting the <u>Cross of Christ</u> as the only way of salvation from sin and uncleanness.

Now, let's go back to John 4. Notice, this Samaritan woman was now face to face with the life-giving one. This one can give her eternal living water.

JOHN 4
Verse 11
The woman saith unto him, Sir, thou hast nothing to draw with, and the well is deep: from whence then hast thou that living water?

Eastern travelers frequently carried leather buckets with which to draw water from public wells. This well was about 105 feet deep, 9 feet in diameter and about had about 15 feet of water in the well. It was cut out of solid rock. No wonder she said to Jesus, "you have nothing to draw with and the well is deep."

Her next question is a very important one. "From whence hast thou that living water?"

Verse 13
Jesus answered and said unto her, whosoever drinketh of this water shall thirst again:

Verse 14
But whosoever drinketh of the water that I shall give him shall never thirst; but the water that I shall give him shall be in him a well of water springing up into everlasting life.

Verse 15
The woman saith unto him, Sir, give me this water, that I thirst not, neither come hither to draw.

JOHN 17
Verse 3
And this is life eternal, that they might know thee the only true God, and Jesus Christ, whom thou hast sent.

Eternal life is more than endless existence. It is a personal relationship with God; to know Him like Adam did is temporary life (Genesis 2:17). Eternal life is not prolonged or eternal continuance of being. For all mankind will have this and will be judged and punished in conscious existence forever. It is not merely eternal existence, but eternal knowing of God in eternal and perfect correspondence and infinite environment. This life is only in God's Son and what He did on the cross. Thus, everlasting life is not merely everlasting existence.

JOHN 4
Verse 16
Jesus saith unto her, Go, call thy husband, and come hither.

Notice, these two verses (John 4:15-16) show a request of the woman and then Jesus gives her two reasons for asking it.

1. This was Christ's way of getting to the rest of her problem (or trouble) so He could give her salvation.
2. He could see her past and He knew her thoughts. She had five different husbands and the one she had now was not her husband.

How often, when Christ through the Holy Spirit convicts our hearts, we quickly change the subject and begin to tell God how and where we worship.

Verse 21
Jesus saith unto her, Woman, believe me, the hour cometh, when ye shall neither in this mountain, nor yet at Jerusalem, worship the Father.

The answer provides a great principle.
The true worship is that of the heart and not of or at any particular place.

Verse 23
But the hour cometh, and now is, when the true worshippers shall worship the Father in spirit and in truth: for the Father seeketh such to worship him.

Verse 24
God is a Spirit: and they that worship him must worship him in spirit and in truth.

Worshipers are to worship with the whole soul, mind, feeling, emotions and desires not bodily actions or journeying to some far temple or church. We often hear of a church that has a great service. We run to it and try to worship there. When it is over we feel so let down. Harmony is with fully revealed and attested truth, not in controversies, rituals and offerings.

God is a spirit not the sun or moon. Not an image of wood or stone, or of beast or man. He is not the air, wind, universal mind, love or some impersonal quality. He is a person with a personal spirit, body and a personal soul. He is like that of man except His body is of spirit substance instead of flesh and bones.

In Verse 24, John gives three descriptions of God:
(1) He is a Spirit; (2) He is love; and (3) He is light. God is a spiritual being who is invisible and with a body. He is a divine person who reveals Himself in perfect intellect, emotion and will. He is self-existent (Genesis 1:1)

HEBREWS 1
Verse 3
Who being the brightness of his glory, and the express image of his person, and upholding all things by the word of his power, when he had by himself purged our sins, sat down on the right hand of the Majesty on high:

Christ's person, power and position are all expressed in this verse. He is described as being "the brightness of God's glory".

The word "being" means existing; whose force is <u>eternally being</u>.

This word guards against Him becoming deity somewhere after His birth.

He was always equal with the Father.

This describes of Him His very nature. They were neither added to nor taken from Him during His earthly ministry.
The "brightness" here spoken of refers to a radiance or a shining forth of divine glory.

As the rays of light are related to the Son with neither one existing apart from the other, so the Father and the Son are essentially one.

The Son is the express image of the Father's person (not nature).

The radiant light implies the oneness of the Son with the Father.

The imprint expresses the distinctness of the Son from the Father, yet oneness and distinctness are implied in each.

JOHN 4
Verse 25
The woman saith unto him, I know that Messias cometh, which is called Christ: when he is come, he will tell us all things.

Verse 26
Jesus saith unto her, I that speak unto thee am he.

Verse 28
The woman then left her water pot, and went her way into the city, and saith to the men,

Verse 29
Come, see a man, which told me all things that ever I did: is not this the Christ?

The disciples marveled because Jesus was talking to a woman. It was forbidden for a Rabbi to talk to a woman in public or instruct them in the law. No Rabbi could even converse with his wife or daughter in public.

It may have been that Christ did tell her about her life so her report was no exaggeration, for she went into the city and told the men what Jesus said unto her.

CHAPTER 5
JESUS, THE GREAT PHYSICAN

JOHN 5
Verse 2
Now there is at Jerusalem by the sheep market (or sheep gate) a pool, which is called in the Hebrew tongue Bethesda (or House of Mercy), having five porches.

Verse 3
In these lay a great multitude of impotent folk (or weak sickly people), of blind, halt (or lame), withered (or paralyzed), waiting for the moving of the water.

Verse 4
For an angel went down at a certain season (or time) into the pool, and troubled (or stirred up) the water: whosoever then first after the troubling of the water stepped in was made whole of whatsoever disease he had.

Verse 5
And a certain man was there, which had an infirmity thirty and eight years.

Verse 6
When Jesus saw him lie, and knew that he had been now a long time in that case (or condition), he saith unto him, Wilt thou be made whole (or Do you want to be healed)?

Verse 7
The impotent (or sick) man answered him, Sir, I have no man, when the water is troubled (or stirred up), to put me into the pool: but while I am coming, another steppeth down before me.

Verse 8
Jesus saith unto him, Rise, take up thy bed, and walk.

Verse 9
And immediately the man was made whole (or well), and took up his bed, and walked: and on the same day was the Sabbath.

Notice, this man had an outstanding day today, for in the next few moments he was going to receive a miracle from a man he never knew or ever met before.

For 38 years he had been like this and the Great Physician knew all about him. He probably was told, "There is no cure for you unless you get in the troubled water of the pool."

Listen now to a question Jesus is about to ask him. "Wilt thou be made whole?" Here was Christ's way of approaching this impotent man. Or in other words, "Do you want to be well?" No doubt this was a foolish question to be asked from a man you didn't know. Jesus always has a way of approaching you when He wants to get your attention, for no one sick would choose to remain sick. The impotent man was waiting in hope somebody would help him into the pool.

Let's look now at the question of Jesus. I believe He was look into the man's inner being, or heart. Have you the will to be healed? This man was placing his remaining condition now on the fact he had no one to put him into the troubled water. He was bound by his circumstances and could rise no higher than his complaint. The sickness of his body was now accompanied by a partial sickness of his will. He felt it was impossible now that no one would help him.

Jesus' selection of this man from a large group at the pool indicated His interest in restoring those who have been reduced to helplessness both in body and in spirit. Here is a man who has laid here for 38 years. Now a man who he does not even know says to him, "Rise, take up [thy bed and walk." This man had just expressed his inability to do anything for himself. This must have sounded like a mocking or making fun of him. But these words were a great challenge to an enfeebled man's will as his sick body.

Let's notice what takes place now. The Jews told him it was unlawful to carry his bed on the Sabbath, for in Verse 11 he told the Jews, "He that made me whole said unto me, Take up thy bed and walk." Next the Jews want to know, "What man said unto thee, take up thy bed and walk?"

The impotent man, who now was made whole, knew not who made him whole. So Jesus had withdrawn from the pool and the multitude who were there. He knew the hatred of the leaders and the result of His breaking of the Jewish law of the Sabbath not to carry a bed on the Sabbath.

JOHN 5
Verse 15
The man departed, and told the Jews that it was Jesus, which had made him whole.

The man had to be reminded who had said unto him, "Take up thy bed and walk."
For 38 years he had to depend on others. Now he must depend on the one who made him whole, for Jesus told him to go and sin no more.

CHAPTER 6
JESUS, THE BREAD OF LIFE

JOHN 6
Verse 31
Our fathers did eat manna in the desert; as it is written, He gave them bread from heaven to eat.

Verse 32
Then Jesus said unto them, Verily, verily, I say unto you, Moses gave you not that bread from heaven; but my Father giveth you the true bread from heaven.

EXODUS 16
Verse 15
And when the children of Israel saw it, they said one to another, It is manna: for they wist not (*or did not know*) what it was. And Moses said unto them, this is the bread which the Lord hat given you to eat.

Manna – meaning "What is it?"

Not only was it remarkable for its size, shape, color and taste, but especially that of its daily appearance at dawn and its tremendous abundance.
It taught the people to look to God for their daily bread, and it was a symbol of the coming bread of Jesus Christ.
Jesus is saying in Verse 32, "Moses did not give you the true bread that feeds the soul and sustains eternal life, but that bread which only sustains and feeds the body only."

JOHN 6
Verse 33
For the bread of God is he which cometh down from heaven, and giveth life unto the world.

Verse 34
Then said they unto him, Lord, evermore give us this bread.

They thought Jesus was still talking about temporal food and looked-for manna or bread.

PROVERBS 30
Verse 8

Remove far from me vanity and lies: give me neither poverty nor riches; feed me with food convenient for me:
The words of Agur here in Proverbs was six requests from the Lord.

1. Deny me not my petitions
2. Remove vanity from me
3. Remove lies from me
4. Give me not poverty
5. Give me not riches
6. Feed me only my necessary food

PHILIPPIANS 4
Verse 19

But my God shall supply <u>all your need</u> according to his riches in glory by Christ Jesus.

This promise is still true for the believers who are in Christ Jesus and who is faithful to God.

JOHN 6
Verse 37

And Jesus said unto them, <u>I am the bread of life</u>: he that cometh to me shall never hunger; <u>and he that believeth</u> on me shall never thirst.

The meaning of "the bread of life" is "the bread which gives life". We saw in Exodus the manna (or bread) only lasts one day and then it bred worms (Exodus 16:20) and stank. Here this bread gives life. Neither will a man thirst again.

JOHN 6
Verse 47
Verily, verily, I say unto you, He that believeth on me hath everlasting life.

Verse 49
Your fathers did eat manna in the wilderness, and are dead.

The manna in the wilderness was not the bread that gives eternal life.

JOHN 6
Verse 50
This is the bread which cometh down from heaven, that a man eat thereof, and not die.

Verse 51
I am the living bread which came down from Heaven: if any man eat of this bread, he shall live forever: and the bread that I will give is my flesh, which I will give for the life of the world.

Notice, eating of Christ's flesh simply means that a believer must accept, by faith, what Christ did for him at the cross and live by obedience to him without sin. The penalty has already been paid.

JOHN 6
Verse 63
It is the spirit that quickeneth; the flesh profiteth nothing: the words that I speak unto you, they are spirit, and they are life.

If you could literally "eat my flesh and drink my blood" it would not save your souls. The life He speaks of is spiritual and eternal.

Verse 53
Then Jesus said unto them, Verily, verily, I say unto you, except ye eat the flesh of the Son of man, and drink his blood, ye have no life in you.

Verse 54
Whoso eateth my flesh, and drinketh my blood, hath eternal life; and I will raise him up at the last day.

Verse 55
For my flesh is meat indeed, and my blood is drink indeed.

Verse 56
He that eateth my flesh, and drinketh my blood, dwelleth in me, and I in him.

Eating and drinking is used figuratively of partaking of the benefits of the death and resurrection of Christ. We take by faith and enjoy His benefits because God gives them unto us according to what Christ did for us.

Verse 58
This is that bread which came down from heaven: not as your fathers did eat manna, and are dead: he that eateth of this bread shall live forever.

Six times in this chapter, Jesus promises everlasting life if they meet certain conditions.

1. May have everlasting life (Verse 40)
2. He that believeth hath everlasting life (Verse 47)
3. May not die (Verse 50)
4. Eat this manna and live forever (Verse 51)
5. Whoso eateth His flesh and drinketh His blood hath eternal or everlasting life (Verse 54)
6. He that eatheth this bread shall live forever (Verse 58)

> ### JOHN 6
> ### Verse 27
> *Labour not for the meat which perisheth, but for that meat which endureth unto everlasting life, which the Son of man shall give unto you: for him hath God the Father sealed.*

Jesus is the real living Bread of Life. Seek to obey Him and you shall have everlasting life and He shall raise you up in the last day.

Remember, Jesus said, "I am the Bread of Life." (JOHN 6 Verse 48)

CHAPTER 7
JESUS, THE WATER OF LIFE

> ### JOHN 7
> ### Verse 37
> *In the last day, that great day of the feast, Jesus stood and cried, saying, if any man thirst, let him come unto me, and drink.*

In order to do this precious scripture justice, we must look back as to why it is so important in the Old Testament to the New Testament.

LEVITICOUS 23
Verse 35
On the first day shall be an holy convocation: ye shall do no servile work therein.

Verse 36ᵃ
Seven days ye shall offer an offering made by fire unto the LORD: on the eighth day shall be an holy convocation unto you; and ye shall offer an offering made by fire unto the LORD: it is a solemn assembly (*or large gathering of people*) …

Notice the Eighth Day…
This was a special day in addition to the seven days of the Feast of Tabernacles. It was a day of solemn assembly and a special Sabbath. The eighth day is as a new beginning.

REVELATION 21
1[(a)]
And I saw a new heaven and a new earth…

Notice, this is because of the renovation of the earth by fire on the eighth day or Holy Convocation. This day of the feast in John 7 was the Eighth Day that Jesus stood and cried, "If any man thirst." This day is the last day of the feast. Now let's watch in the Old Testament.

The eighth day was the day of assembly offering sacrifices for Israel. The first seven days they offered sacrifices for the nations. But on this last day a priest would draw water from the pool of Siloam in the <u>golden vessel</u> and would bring it to the temple, and at that time of <u>the morning sacrifice while it was on the alter</u> he would pour this water, mingled with wine, upon it. It probably was at this time of the assembly that Jesus cried, "Come unto me and drink." The prophecy or symbol of Leviticus 23 was being fulfilled, for this was about the Holy Spirit that Jesus was talking about to each believer in Him.

This confirms the fact that any man and generation from the beginning of the fulfillment of this prophecy can experience the Holy Spirit or <u>River of Living Water</u>.

LEVITICUS 24
Verse 1
And the Lord Spake unto Moses, saying

Verse 2
Command the children of Israel that they bring unto thee <u>pure oil</u> olive beaten for the light, to cause the lamps to burn continually.

Verse 3
Without the vail of the testimony, in the tabernacle of the congregation, shall Aaron order it from the evening unto the morning before the LORD continually: it shall be a statute forever in your generations?

Verse 5
And thou shalt take fine flour, and bake twelve cakes thereof: two tenth deals shall be in one cake.

Verse 6
And thou shalt set them in two rows, six on a row, upon the pure table before the LORD.

Verse 7
And thou shalt put pure <u>frankincense</u> upon each row that it may be on the bread for a memorial, even an offering made by fire unto the LORD.

God had told Moses to command the children of Israel to bring pure oil beaten for the light.

Beaten Oil – was made by bruising the olives in a mill without the application of heat. Other oil, or inferior oil, could be made under stronger pressure and with the aid of heat.

ISAIAH 53
Verse 5
But he was wounded for our transgressions, he was bruised for our iniquities: the chastisement of our peace was upon him; and with his stripes we are healed.

The stacks of show bread were placed upon the <u>pure table</u>. This was a table with <u>pure gold</u> that stood before the Lord. Also, <u>pure frankincense</u> was to be burned upon the <u>pure table</u>. This signifies that all things connected with Jehovah and His worship were to be <u>pure</u> (thus typifying the purity of life and conduct of the worshipers.

Now let's return to John 7, Verse 37 and watch what happens.

1. It confirms that any man of every race and generation from the beginning to the fulfillment of the prophecy can experience the Holy Spirit.
2. He that believeth – proves that the promise is for everyone, for He said, "If <u>any</u> man thirst".

Tarry – meaning stay or remain.
Now watch this very closely...

HABAKKUK 2
Verse 3
For the vision is yet for an appointed time, but at the end it shall speak, and not lie: though it <u>tarry</u>, wait for it; because it will surely come, it will not tarry.

JOEL 2
Verse 28
And it shall come to pass afterward, that I will pour out my spirit upon all flesh; and your sons and your daughters shall prophesy, your old men shall dream dreams, your young men shall see visions:

Jesus said just before His ascension...

LUKE 24
Verse 49
And, behold, I send the promise of my Father upon you: but tarry ye in the city of Jerusalem, until ye be endued with power from on high.

The promise is to all mankind who are believers. But tarry. This is what the disciples were told to do to get the Baptism or the well of living water from on high to do the works of Christ.

Endued – Greek word enduo, (Strong's 1746) in the sense of sinking into a garment, to put on.

1. To put on – Matthew 27:31
2. Be clothed with – Mark 15:17
3. Be clothed in – Revelation 15:6
4. Be arrayed in – Acts 12:21

Anyone clothed with this power will be able to confirm what he preaches.

Power – Greek word dunamis (Strong's # 1411) meaning miraculous power.

The enduement of power is the same as receiving the promise of the Father or the promise of the Holy Spirit in baptismal measurement. Power to do the works of Christ is what was promised.

JOHN 14
Verse 12
Verily, verily, I say unto you, He that believeth on me, the works that I do shall he do also; and greater works than these shall he do; because I go unto my Father.

Verse 13
And whatsoever ye shall ask in my name, that will I do, that the Father may be glorified in the Son.

Verse 14
If ye shall ask <u>any thing in my name</u>, I will do it.

The purpose of the Christian's <u>power</u> of attorney – It glorifies God, to answer prayers to save, heal and bless all men. But He can only do this if they ask in faith, nothing wavering.

JAMES 1
Verse 6[a]
But let him ask in faith, nothing wavering (*not wavering*).

Let's see what else these verses in John reveals.

JOHN 7
Verse 38
He that believeth on me, as the scripture hath said, out of his belly shall flow rivers of living water.

Verse 39
(But this spake he of the Spirit, which they that believe on him should receive: for the Holy Ghost was not yet given; because that Jesus was not yet glorified.)

Notice

There are conditions of receiving the Spirit of the Lord.

1. Thirst – this means to have a craving and passion of the soul to have full and complete union with God and the fullness of the Spirit
2. Come unto me – means the complete surrender of the life to do the whole will of God <u>as light is received.</u>
3. Drink – means the whole-hearted reception into one's life the gifts, the fruit and operation of the Holy Spirit.
4. Believe on me as the scripture hath said – this means to believe and obey the whole gospel of Christ

<u>Believe on me</u> = faith – means confidence in the testimony of another

1. To be persuaded of "things which are not as though they are" (Romans 4:17)
2. To place confidence in (Ephesians 3:12)

3. The substance of hope and the assurance of things not seen (Hebrews 11:1)
4. Dependence upon and reliance in the word of God (Matthew 15:28)
5. Full surrender and obedience to all known truth (Romans 6:11-23)
6. Trust wholly in the faithfulness of God (Matthew 6:25-34)
7. Give one's self over to a new way of life (Romans 8:1-16)
8. The attribute of God and restored man can bring into existence things that are unseen to things that are seen (Romans 4:17)
9. The whole body of revealed truth (I Timothy 4:1; Jude 3)
10. Joyful faith in acceptance of Christ as the substitute for sin and our savior (Romans 1:16)
    a. Access into grace (Romans 5:2)
    b. Fulfillment of the promise (Hebrews 6:12)
    c. The Holy Spirit (Galatians 3:14)
    d. Righteousness (Romans 9:30; Romans 10:6)
    e. Sonship (Galatians 3:26)
    f. Healing (I Peter 2:24)
    g. Eternal life (John 3:15-16)
    h. Answers to one's prayers (Matthew 7:7-8)

These are the explanations of the Rivers of Living Water that Jesus spoke of. This river became fulfilled on the great day of Pentecost. The river became a reality in Acts 2. Remember what Habakkuk 2:3 says "though it tarry wait for it because it will surely come."

ACTS 2
Verse 1
And when the day of Pentecost was fully come, they were all with one accord in one place.

Pentecost – means 50 days after the resurrection of Christ

LEVITICUS 23
Verse 15
And ye shall count unto you from the morrow after the Sabbath, from the day that ye brought the sheaf of the wave offering; seven Sabbaths shall be complete:

Verse 16
Even unto the morrow after the seventh Sabbath shall ye number fifty days; and ye shall offer a new meat offering unto the LORD.

LUKE 24
Verse 49
And, behold, I send the promise of my Father upon you: but tarry ye in the city of Jerusalem, until ye be endued with power from on high.

Notice, this is not an afterthought of the Father. It is a part of God's eternal will. "Endued" conveys a picture of one being clothed with God's enablement.

Our last thing we want to mention about the river of living water is in preparation for battle.

Armor – meaning –
1. A defensive covering used in battle
2. That which gives the Christian protection and confidence

EPHESIANS 6
Verse 11
Put on the whole armour of God that ye may be able to stand against the wiles of the devil.

Armor – meaning –
1. Ability to stand against enemies
2. Ability to withstand attacks
3. Ability to quench the fiery darts of Satan

Wiles of Satan – (Strong's 3180 – methadeia) – meaning trickery (wile); to lie in wait; the schemes used to deceive, entrap, enslave and ruin the souls of men

Wrestle – refers to warfare in general between saints and spirit rebels who are against God.

There are seven different aspects to the Christian armor.
1. Loins girt about with truth (Ephesians 6:14)
2. Breastplate of righteousness (Ephesians 6:14)
3. Feet shot with the gospel of peace (Ephesians 6:15)
4. The shield of faith (Ephesians 6:16)
5. The helmet of salvation (Ephesians 6:17)
6. The sword of the Spirit (or Word of God) (Ephesians 6:17)

The last one makes it all possible...
7. Praying always and watching (Ephesians 6:18)

These are of great importance to be given by the Holy Spirit. Then a true river of living water can flow.

Now...

GALATIANS 5
Verse 16
This I say then, <u>Walk in the Spirit</u>, and <u>ye shall not</u> fulfil the lust of the flesh.

The nine-fold fruit of the spirit...
1. Love – a strong compassion to the well-being of another person (I Corinthians 13:4)
2. Joy – delight over blessings for self and others (I Peter 1-8)
3. Peace – the state of trust (Philippians 4:7)
4. Long suffering – to bear long with patience (II Corinthians 6:4)
5. Gentleness – mildness combined with tenderness (II Timothy 2:24)
6. Goodness – God-like in conduct (Matthew 5:44)
7. Faith – absolute dependence on the word of God (Hebrews 11:1)
8. Meekness – to be kind and not harboring resentment (Titus 3:2)
9. Temperance – self control of passions (Romans 13:14; Galatians 6:24)

We see how important the whole armor of God is to the believer. When you flow in the living waters you can also think on these things...

PHILIPPIANS 4
Verse 8
Finally, brethren, whatsoever things are true, whatsoever things are honest, whatsoever things are just, whatsoever things are pure, whatsoever things are lovely, whatsoever things are of good report; if there be any virtue, and if there be any praise, think on these things.

1. True – all that is in harmony with the word of God (2 Timothy 2:15; 2 Timothy 3:16-17)
2. Honest – all that is decent and honorable to the Christian (2 Timothy 3:8; Titus 2:2)
3. Just – all that is in harmony with righteousness (2 Peter 1: 4-10; Romans 3:25-27)
4. Pure – all that is chaste and holy for body and soul (I Corinthians 3:16-17; 2 Corinthians 7:1)
5. Lovely – all things that are pleasing and will be pleasing to and tends to bless others (I Corinthians 13:4-8)
6. Good Report – all that is in harmony with the best public good; virtuous and praiseworthy
(Romans 13:1-10)

Every true child of God that is flowing in the living water of this Great chapter of John should be ever thankful for the precious Heavenly Guest. Much could be added about John 7:37-39. The scripture is very precious about the Third Person of the Trinity.

There are 27 different books in the New Testament and each one has a different aspect or name for the Heavenly Guest.

1. Matthew 1:18 – He is the one who begot the child Jesus through Mary.
2. Mark 1:10 – He is the Anointer
3. Luke 3:22 – He is the identifier of Christ
4. John 14:16 – He is our helper
5. Acts 2:4 – He is our infiller
6. Romans 8:14 – He is our proof of sonship to God
7. I Corinthians 12:7-11 – He is the giver of spiritual gifts
8. 2Corinthians 3:7-18 – He is the glory of the New Covenant
9. Galatians 5:22-23 – He is the producer of spiritual fruit
10. Ephesians 4:1-6 – He is the unity of the Church in the bond of peace
11. Philippians – He is the fellowship of the believers
12. Colossians 3:16 – He is our spiritual song
13. I Thessalonians 1:5 – He is the power and assurance of the Gospel
14. 2 Thessalonians 2:13 – He is defender against lawlessness and apostasy
15. I Timothy 4:1 – He is the defender of our faith and doctrine
16. 2 Timothy 1:13-14 – He is the keeper of sound works of faith
17. Titus 3:5 – He is our cleansing, renewing and regeneration
18. Philemon 1:17 – He is the restorer of relationship
19. Hebrews 9:8 – He is the entrance to the Holy Place
20. James 2:26 – He is the empowerer of the work of faith
21. I Peter 1:11-12 – He is the glorifier of Christ and the anointer of preachers
22. 2 Peter 1:21 – He is the Inspirer and giver of the Holy Scriptures

23. I John 2:20-23 – He is the revealer of Christ and the Antichrist
24. 2vJohn 1:4-5 – He is the energizer of love
25. 3 John 1:4 – He is the energizer of truth
26. Jude 1: 20 – He empowers the prayers of the saints
27. Revelation 4:2 – He is the one who ushers us into the presence of God

CHAPTER 8
JESUS, THE DEFENDER OF THE WEAK

JOHN 8

Verse 3

And the scribes and Pharisees brought unto him a <u>woman taken in adultery</u>; *and when they had set her in the midst,*

Verse 4

They say unto him, Master, this woman was taken in adultery, in the very act.

Verse 5

<u>*Now*</u> *Moses in the law commanded us, that such should be stoned: but what sayest thou?*

Verse 6

This they said, <u>*tempting him*</u> *that they might have to accuse him. But Jesus stooped down, and with his* <u>*finger wrote on the ground*</u>, *as though he heard them not.*

Verse 7

So, when they continued asking him, he lifted up himself, and said unto them, <u>*He that is without sin among you*</u>, *let him first cast a stone at her.*

Verse 8

And again, he stooped down, and wrote on the ground.

Verse 9

And they which heard it, being <u>*convicted by their own conscience*</u>, *went out one by one, beginning at the eldest, even unto the last: and Jesus was* <u>*left alone*</u>, *and the woman standing in the midst.*

Verse 10

When Jesus had lifted up himself, and saw none but the woman, he said unto her, Woman, where are those thine <u>*accusers*</u>? *Hath no man condemned thee?*

Verse 11

She said, No man, Lord. And Jesus said unto her, neither do I condemn thee: go, and sin no more.

We must see what the Law says about adultery.

The Law...

EXODUS 20
Verse 14
Thou shalt not commit adultery.

This commandment prohibits <u>all</u> unlawful sexual relationship and upholds the sacredness of marriage.

LEVITICUS 20
Verse 10
(Death for Adultery)
And the man that committeth adultery with another man's wife, even he that committeth adultery with his neighbour's wife, the adulterer and the adulteress shall surely be put to death.

DEUTERONOMY 22
Verse 21
Then they shall bring out the damsel to the door of her father's house, and the men of her city shall stone her with stones that she die: <u>because she hath wrought folly in Israel, to play the whore in her father's house</u>: so shalt thou put evil away from among you.

Verse 22
If a man be found lying with a woman married to an husband, then they shall both of them die, both the man that lay with the woman, and the woman: so shalt thou put away evil from Israel.

Verse 23
<u>If a damsel</u> that is a virgin be betrothed unto an husband, and a man find her in the city, and lie with her;

Verse 24
Then ye shall bring them both out unto the gate of that city, and ye shall stone them with stones that they die; the damsel, <u>because she cried not</u>, being in the city; and <u>the man, because he hath</u> humbled his neighbour's wife: so, thou shalt put away evil from among you.

There are three commands for <u>Rape and Adultery</u>

1. If a damsel (or virgin) be found guilty of losing her virginity before her marriage, the elders of the city shall bring her before the door of her father's house and all the men of her city shall <u>kill her with stones.</u> (Deuteronomy 22:21)
2. If a man be found lying with a married woman <u>they both shall be killed</u> (Deuteronomy 22:22)
3. If a man finds a betrothed virgin in the city and lies with her, they shall both be stoned to death in the gate of the city. (Deuteronomy 22:23-24)

There are four death penalties for these sins

1. Forfeiting virginity before marriage (Deuteronomy 22:21)
2. Adultery with a married woman (Deuteronomy 22:22)
3. Raping a betrothed woman in the city (Deuteronomy 22:23-24)
4. Raping a betrothed woman in the field (Deuteronomy 22:25-27)

We now see the Law and the penalties. The Scribes and Pharisees now were tempting Jesus by asking, "What sayest thou?" The Law required the man to be brought there as one of the accusers and there must be at least two or three witnesses to convict a man.

DEUTERONOMY 17
Verse 6
At the mouth of two witnesses, or three witnesses, shall he that is worthy of death be put to death; but at the mouth of <u>one</u> witness he shall not be put to death.

DEUTERONOMY 19
Verse 15
One witness shall not rise up against a man for any iniquity, or for any sin, in any sin that he sinneth: at the mouth of two witnesses, or at the mouth of three witnesses, shall the matter be established.

Jesus knew the Law and therefore if He had contradicted Moses' Law, He would have been a false prophet. Also, if He had have condemned the woman to death, He would have been accused of using the

Romans as usurping authority.
Instead, He stooped to the ground and merely wrote as though He never heard them.

When they continued to ask Jesus, He said unto them, "Let him that is without <u>sin</u> cast the first stone." What Jesus wrote on the ground is unknown, but it brought conviction on their part.

There are six causes of causes of conviction

The word conviction means "making one conscious of his guilt". In John 8:9, they were convicted by their own conscious.

1. Their own evil design against Jesus and not so much against her
2. Their failure to include the man who was guilty as much as the woman
3. What Jesus wrote on the ground
4. The challenge to start throwing stones if they were sinless themselves
5. Their hypocrisy which was known to Christ and others
6. Their guilt of committing the same sin

ROMANS 2
Verse 1
Therefore, thou art <u>inexcusable</u>, O man, whosoever thou art that judgest: for wherein thou judgest another, <u>thou condemnest thyself</u>; for thou that judgest doest the same things.

Jesus knew the law about the witnessing against anyone.
Jesus then asked the woman this question, "Where are those thine accusers?
Hath no man condemned thee?" She replied, "No man Lord." And Jesus said unto her, "Neither do I condemn thee, go and sin no more." Jesus also knew that the testimony of one was not enough to convict her.

JOHN 5
Verse 31
If I bear witness of myself, my witness is not true.

Early Christians thought Jesus was not condemning adultery here, but the idea is that He was not a magistrate and since no man of her accusers stayed to condemn her, He was not going to pass sentence upon her, taking it upon Himself to execute the Law of Moses. Christ had to avoid the Jews accusing Him of taking authority in His own hands.

Then too, Christ came to save men not to destroy them, so forgiveness of her sins was an obligation of His, as it is today when anyone repents and turns from sins.

I JOHN 1
Verse 9
If we confess our sins, he is faithful and just to forgive us our sins, and to cleanse us from all unrighteousness.

This precious sacrifice

There are four things God will do...
1. Be faithful to us
2. Be just with us
3. Forgive our sins
4. Cleanse us from all unrighteousness

Jesus did not say he did not condemn adultery as a sin. He simply forgave the woman as He had done others who were sinful (Matthew 9:1-8; Luke 7:37-50). He told her to sin no more, proving He did condemn the adultery as sin. He did elsewhere in Matthew 5:27-32 and Matthew 19:9.

JOHN 3
Verse 16
For God so loved the world, that he gave his only begotten Son, that whosoever believeth in him should not perish, but have everlasting life.

Verse 17
For God sent not his Son into the world to condemn the world; but that the world through him might be saved.

Everlasting – meaning eternal, lasting throughout all time or unknown time, time out of mind, eternity, time without end. The life itself is eternal. Man's possession of it does not change its nature or existence. It is eternal whether man loses it or not. It always remains eternal and is only in Jesus Christ.

MARK 8
Verse 37
Or what shall a man give in exchange for his soul?

CHAPTER 9
JESUS THE LIGHT OF THE WORLD

> ### JOHN 9
> ### Verse 1
> *And as Jesus passed by, he saw a man which was blind from his birth.*

Once again Jesus has mercy on a very special case. The disciples ask a question, "Who did sin, this man or his parents that he was born blind?" Watch what Jesus answered them, saying, "Neither hath this man sinned nor his parents. But that the works of God should be made manifest."

This man was called a beggar in Verse 8. He had been dependant on the generosity of others for support. He was unproductive in the community and contributing nothing. He was a mere nuisance to the people. Here was a man who needed a miracle.

Notice, the motive for a cure was Christ and His compassion. Jesus had little to gain by healing this blind man. He needed no further healing to show his power.

> ### Verse 5
> *As long as I am in the world, I am the light of the world.*
>
> ### Verse 6
> *When he had thus spoken, he spat on the ground, and made clay of the spittle, and he anointed the eyes of the blind man with the clay,*

In Verse 5 Jesus states, "While I am in the world I am the Light of the world." This blind man, no doubt, wondered about this man whom he never saw before. Now He was applying spittle and clay to his eyes, which never had seen anything or anyone.

> ### Verse 7
> *And said unto him, Go, wash in the pool of Siloam, (which is by interpretation, Sent.) He went his way therefore, and washed, and came seeing.*

These words must have been very hard to understand; a blind man with spittle and clay on his eyes. And now to walk to the pool and wash. No doubt even if he wondered about the part of seeing, he no doubt wanted to go and wash the spittle and clay from his eyes. The clay had no medical purpose but rather to provide the man with Christ's intent.

MATTHEW 4
Verse 16[(a)]
The people which sat in darkness saw great light;

Light

The undivided and absolute light. The opposite of all darkness. Therefore, especially used of God.

TIMOTHY 6
Verse 16
Who only hath immortality, dwelling in the <u>light</u> which no man can approach unto; whom no man hath seen, nor can see: to whom be honour and power everlasting. <u>Amen</u>.

The true light of God dwells in infinite Glory which no man has ever seen nor can see. Moses talked with God face to face out of His Glory and when he requested "Show me thy Glory." It could not be granted except as manifested through the back or hinder parts of God. (Exodus 33:11-12)

Here, this beggar which sat in darkness is about to see great light.

JOHN 9
Verse 8
The neighbours therefore, and they which before had seen him that he was blind, said, is not this he that sat and begged?

Verse 9
Some said, this is he: others said, He is like him: but he said, <u>I am he</u>.

The man's eyes were a miracle of now seeing and it. They all acknowledged...
1. He was born blind
2. The man who could now see was identified
3. That he could now see

Neither error or fraud could be seen. Let's look at what happens next to try his faith.

JOHN 9
Verse 18
But the Jews did not believe concerning him, that he had been blind, and received his sight, <u>until</u> they called the parents of him that had received his sight.

Verse 19
And they asked them, saying, is this your son, who ye say was born blind? How then doth he now see?

Verse 20
His parents answered them and said, we know that this is our son, and that he was born blind:

Notice

This miracle could not be a mistaken identity. His parents acknowledged that it was indeed their son.

Verse 21

But by what means he now seeth, we know not; or who hath opened his eyes, we know not: he is of age; ask him: he shall speak for himself.

They ask a question, "How can this man that is a sinner heal the blind?" Why could not the Pharisees heal the blind man if they were more of God than He? The blind sinner was more sensible than all the religious leaders of the day, for only one miracle and one brief contact with this man and he know that He was a prophet.

This is why they were so blind, they would not believe facts when they were seen. They would not believe that He was a prophet, which according to the Jews themselves, permitted one to
Break the Sabbath.

Verse 22

These words spake his parents, because they feared the Jews: for the Jews had agreed already, that if any man did confess that he was Christ, he should be put out of the synagogue.

Verse 23

Therefore, said his parents, He is of age; ask him.

Too many parents, if membership is involved, will not stand up for truth and righteousness. Anyone acknowledging Jesus as the Messiah would be cut off from all religious worship.

Verse 24

Then again called they the man that was blind, and said unto him, Give God the praise: we know that this man is a sinner.

Verse 25

He answered and said, whether he be a sinner or no, I know not: one thing I know, that, whereas I was blind, now I see.

Verse 26

Then said they to him again, what did he to thee? How opened he thine eyes?

Verse 27

He answered them, I have told you already, and ye did not hear: wherefore would ye hear it again? Will ye also be his disciples?

They were words of an oath. To give God praise was equivalent of swearing to tell the truth.

JOSHUA 7
Verse 19
And Joshua said unto Achan, My son, give, I pray thee, glory to the LORD God of Israel, and make confession unto him; and tell me now what thou hast done; hide it not from me.

While they sought to put him under oath, an oath they put their own words in his mouth to say that Jesus was a sinner, the man answered wisely. This is the third time the man blind was asked the same question. The blind man was the only one who stood up to the Pharisees.

LUKE 11
Verse 34
The light of the body is the eye: therefore, when thine eye is single, thy whole body also is full of light; but when thine eye is evil, thy body also is full of darkness.

MATTHEW 6
Verse 22
The light of the body is the eye: if therefore thine eye be single; thy whole body shall be full of light.

Notice, the light is a lamp filled with oil and gives light to the whole body. If the eye is single and sound and free from lusts, the whole body will be free from sin. Light and darkness are used to contrast knowledge.

2 PETER 2
Verse 14
Having eyes full of adultery, and that cannot cease from sin; beguiling unstable souls: an heart they have exercised with covetous practices; cursed children:

The image of sinful acts are continually floating before their eyes. They reveal imaginations of lustful acts. They seduce the innocent, inexperienced, light and trifling women and also men to surrender their chastity.

The blind man could now see and what a light he shined.

Will you also be his disciple?

(Amen)

CHAPTER 10

JESUS, THE GOOD SHHERD

Meaning "one who tends sheep"

JOHN 10
Verse 11
I am the good shepherd: the good shepherd giveth his life for the sheep.

DUTIES

Duties of the shepherd towards his flock…

Defend

I SAMUEL 17
Verse 34
And David said unto Saul, Thy servant kept his father's sheep, and there came a lion, and a bear, and took a lamb out of the flock:

Verse 35
And I went out after him, and smote him, and delivered it out of his mouth: and when he arose against me, I caught him by his beard, and smote him, and slew him.

Verse 36
Thy servant slew both the lion and the bear: and this uncircumcised Philistine shall be as one of them, seeing he hath defied the armies of the living God.

Verse 37
David said moreover, The LORD that delivered me out of the paw of the lion, and out of the paw of the bear, he will deliver me out of the hand of this Philistine. And Saul said unto David, Go, and the LORD be with thee.

Notice David's great words as a shepherd taking care of his father's sheep. He had been victorious over a lion and a bear. Now he considered the armies of the Lord as his father's sheep and willingly faced this giant. The lad pleaded his case before Saul and said the Lord delivered the lion and the bear into his hands and He will would now deliver him from this Philistine.

There is a five-fold armor of David.

1. The shepherd's staff
2. Five smooth stones from the brook
3. His shepherd's bag
4. His sling in his hand
5. Faith in God

There are six things David predicted.

1. This day the Lord will deliver you into m hands
2. I will smite you
3. I will take your head off
4. I will give the bodies of the Philistines to the birds and beasts this day
5. All this assembly shall know God does not save by carnal means
6. He will give you into my hands

David acknowledges two major truths.
1. There is no God in all the earth like the Lord God of Israel
2. That men may know the Lord God does not save by carnal means

Next a good shepherd must water the flock.

Water

GENESIS 29
Verse 2
And he looked, and behold a well in the field, and, lo, there were three flocks of sheep lying by it; for out of that well they watered the flocks: and a great stone was upon the well's mouth.

Verse 3
And thither were all the flocks gathered: and they rolled the stone from the well's mouth, and watered the sheep, and put the stone again upon the well's mouth in his place.

Verse 4
And Jacob said unto them, my brethren, whence be ye? And they said, Of Haran are we.

Verse 5
And he said unto them, Know ye Laban the son of Nahor? And they said, we know him.

Verse 6
And he said unto them, is he well? And they said, He is well: and, behold, Rachel his daughter cometh with the sheep.

Verse 7
And he said, lo, it is yet high day, neither is it time that the cattle should be gathered together: water ye the sheep, and go and feed them.

Give Rest

JEREMIAH 33
Verse 12
Thus, saith the Lᴏʀᴅ of hosts; again, in this place, which is desolate without man and without beast, and in all the cities thereof, shall be an habitation of shepherds causing their flocks to lie down.

Verse 13
In the cities of the mountains, in the cities of the vale, and in the cities of the south, and in the land of Benjamin, and in the places about Jerusalem, and in the cities of Judah, shall the flocks pass again under the hands of him that telleth (*or counts*) them, saith the Lᴏʀᴅ.

Know Them

JOHN10
Verse 3
To him the porter openeth; and the sheep hear his voice: and he calleth his own sheep by name, and leadeth them out.

Verse 4
And when he putteth forth his own sheep, he goeth before them, and the sheep follow him: for they know his voice.

Verse 5
And a stranger will they not follow, but will flee from him: for they know not the voice of strangers.

Secure Pasture for Them

I CHRONICLES 4
Verse 39
And they went to the entrance of Gedor, even unto the east side of the valley, to <u>seek pasture for their flocks</u>.

Verse 40
And they found fat pasture and good, and the land was wide, and quiet, and peaceable; for they of Ham had dwelt there of old.

EZEKIEL 33
Verse 11
Say unto them, As I live, saith the Lord Gᴏᴅ, I have no pleasure in the death of the wicked; but that the wicked turn from his way and live: turn ye, turn ye from your evil ways; for why will ye die, O house of Israel?

Verse 12
Therefore, thou son of man, say unto the children of thy people, The righteousness of the righteous shall not deliver him in the day of his transgression: as for the wickedness of the wicked, he shall not fall thereby in the

day that he turneth from his wickedness; neither shall the righteous be able to live for his righteousness in the day that he sinneth.

Verse 15
If the wicked restore the pledge, give again that he had robbed, walk in the statutes of life, without committing iniquity; he shall surely live, he shall not die.

PSALMS 23
Verse 1
The LORD is my shepherd; I shall not want.

Verse 2
He maketh me to lie down in green pastures: he leadeth me beside the still waters.

Verse 3
He restoreth my soul: he leadeth me in the paths of righteousness for his name's sake.

Verse 4
Yea, though I walk through the valley of the shadow of death, I will fear no evil: for thou art with me; thy rod and thy staff they comfort me.

Verse 5
Thou preparest a table before me in the presence of mine enemies: thou anointest my head with oil; my cup runneth over.

Verse 6
Surely goodness and mercy shall follow me all the days of my life: and I will dwell in the house of the LORD for ever.

This Psalm is also called the Shepherd of John 10. Here we have the sheep experiencing the more abundant life provided for them by the Messiah or the Good Shepherd. All of the above duties of the shepherd are wrapped up in this Psalm.

1. defend
2. water
3. give rest
4. number
5. know
6. secure pasture
7. search for the lost

There are 14 blessings that the Good Shepherd gives his sheep.
1. The Lord is their Shepherd (Verse 1)
2. No want (verse 1 and Psalms 34:9-10)
3. Rest in green pastures (verse 2)
4. Guidance to still deep waters (verse 2)
5. Restoration of soul (verse 3)

6. Guidance in paths which give no cause for stumbling or going astray (verse 3)
7. Safe passage through the valley of the shadow of death; deep waters; gloomy lands; wild beasts; infested, rocky, dangerous or death-lurking ravines that are so common (verse 4)
8. No fear of evil because of companionship of the shepherd's watchful eye and protection (verse 4)
9. The comfort of the shepherd's rod and staff carried for defense and protection (verse 4)
10. Prepared full table of food to feast on. They feast in safety while the shepherd watches (verse 5)
11. Heads anointed with oil (verse 5)
12. Cups running over not only with food but also plenty of wholesome drink (verse 5)
13. Confidence that goodness and mercy will follow to the end of life (verse 6)
14. Faith that they will dwell in God's house forever (verse 6)

The Good Shepherd takes care of his sheep. There is something special about this chapter about the door or the gate.

JOHN 10
Verse 11
I am the good shepherd: the good shepherd giveth his life for the sheep.

I want to take you to a beautiful picture of this scripture.

Nehemiah, Chapter 3:
1. The sheep gate (verse 1)
   This speaks of the cross (John 10:11)
2. The fish gate (Verse 3)
   This speaks of soul winning (Matthew 4:19)
3. The old gate (verse 6)
   This speaks of the old nature (Romans 6:1-23)
4. The valley gate (verse 13)
   This speaks of suffering and testings (II Corinthians 1:3-5)
5. The dung gate (verse 14)
   This speaks of the flesh (Galatians 5:6-21)
6. The fountain gate (Verse 15)
   This speaks of the Holy Spirit (John 7:37-39)
7. The water gate (verse 26)
   This speaks of the word of God (John 4:10-14)
8. The horse gate (verse26)
   This speaks of the believers' warfare (Ephesians 6:10-19)
9. The east gate (verse29)
   This speaks of the return of Christ (Ephesians 43:1-2)
10. The Miphkad gate (verse 31)
    This was the judgment gate and therefore speaks of the judgment seat of Christ (I Corinthians 3:9-15; II Corinthians 5:10)

It is so wonderful to see all of the gates and what they represent to the Good Shepherd or the Lord Jesus Christ.

> **JOHN 10**
>
> **Verse 14**
>
> *I am the good shepherd, and know my sheep, and am known of mine.*
>
> **Verse 15**
>
> *As the Father knoweth me, even so know I the Father: and I lay down my life for the sheep.*
>
> **Verse 16**
>
> *And other sheep I have, which are not of this fold: them also I must bring, and they shall hear my voice; and there shall be one-fold, and one shepherd.*
>
> **Verse 17**
>
> *Therefore, doth my Father love me, because I lay down my life, that I might take it again?*
>
> **Verse 18**
>
> *No man taketh it from me, but I lay it down of myself. I have power to lay it down, and I have power to take it again. This commandment have I received of my Father.*

LUKE 15

Verse 4

What man of you, having an hundred sheep, if he lose one of them, doth not leave the ninety and nine in the wilderness, and go after that which is lost, until he fined it?

Verse 5

And when he hath found it, he layeth it on his shoulders, rejoicing.

Verse 6

And when he cometh home, he calleth together his friends and neighbours, saying unto them, rejoice with me; for I have found my sheep which was lost.

The Lost Sheep...

1. The shepherd's (or seeker's) loss (verse 4)
2. The shepherd (or seeker) seeks diligently (verse 4)
3. The shepherd's (or seeker's) persistence until found (verse 4)
4. The shepherd's (or seeker's) love (brings back) (verse 5)
5. The shepherd's (or seeker's) joy (rejoicing) (verse 6)
6. The shepherd's (or seeker's) fellowship (called his friends and neighbors to rejoice) (verses 6 & 7)

Before we close this chapter, I want to show you something very special about John 10:15b, "I lay down my life for the sheep."

Notice

The Good Shepherd lays down his life for the sheep. This means that the Great I Am let's Himself become identified with the limitations of self-consciousness that it may lift us up to a spiritual plain. Jesus said, "I lay it down that I might take it again." When we open the door of the mind by consciously affirming the presence and power of the Great I am or Jesus, the Good Shepherd. On our midst, there is a mirage (or vision) of the Heavenly forces with the human being. We find that we are quickened in every part. The life of the I Am having been poured out for us. Thus, Christ becomes Savior of the world by pouring His blood into human consciousness, which each must receive himself and identify himself with.

The Great I Am is the only door through which it can get into our hearts. If it came another way, it is by a thief and a robber. There is but one life giver and savior, the Christ, and the only door through which the divine indwelling can come to us is through the Great I Am. Jesus Christ of Nazareth is the one who points the way, but everyone must take up his cross and follow Him. He said, "My sheep hear my voice and they follow me. A stranger's voice they will not follow."

REVELATION 3
Verse 20
Behold, I stand at the door, and knock: <u>if any man</u> hear my voice, and open the door, I will come in to him, and will sup with him, and he with me.

Verse 21
To him that overcometh will I grant <u>to sit with me</u> in my throne, even as I also overcame, and am set down with my Father in his throne?

If we are faithful to the Great Shepherd who laid down his life and raised it again the third day, if we are overcomers as He overcame, there are 18 great blessings accounted to our account.

1. The Tree of Life (Revelation 2:7)
2. The Crown of Life (Revelation 2:10; 3:11)
3. Escape the second death or lake of fire (Revelation 2:11; 20:14)
4. The hidden manna (Revelation 2:17)
5. The white stone and a new name (Revelation 2:17
6. Part in the Rapture (Revelation 2:25; 3:11; I Timothy 4:16; Philippians 3:21; Colossians 3:4; I Corinthians 15:23; 15:58)
7. Power over nations (revelation 2:26-27)
8. Complete defeat of rebels (Revelation 2:27)
9. The Morning Star (Revelation 2:28)
10. Walk with Christ in white (Revelation 3:4-5)
11. Name eternally in Book of Life (Revelation 3:5; 22:18-19)
12. Confession of name before God (Revelation 3:5)
13. A pillar in God's temple (Revelation 3:12)
14. Eternal abiding with God (Revelation 3:12)
15. God's name upon him (Revelation 3:12)
16. Name of New Jerusalem on him (Revelation 3:12)
17. New name of Christ on him (Revelation 3:12)
18. Eternal throne and kingdom (Revelation 3:21; 1:6; 22:4-5)

Christ is the Good Shepherd and also the <u>Door</u> in John 10:9 He states, "I am the door." Christ is the door and as we enter in we are saved. It is <u>only</u> through Him that we have access unto the Father (Ephesians 2:18). The door is parallel to that of the strait gate and narrow way (Matthew 7:13-14). We cannot narrow the door nor can we widen it. Christ is the door for all mankind. Christ is the door and we cannot go out except across His blood. No ravening wolf can reach those sheep in the sheepfold. No man can pluck them out of His hand
(John 10:28-29)

As the door, Jesus himself preserves and protects his sheep. They can go in and out and find pasture.
Entering in, we find rest
(Psalms 23:2)

To go in and out...shows the sheep have access of the house because they are a family.

DEUTERONOMY 28
Verse 6
Blessed shalt thou be when thou comest in, and blessed shalt thou be when thou goest out.

As Jesus is the door, on which side of it are you?
In Christ or without Christ?
Remember the little song… "One door and only one,
Yet its sides are two.
Inside or outside, Which side are you?

Thank God for the Good Shepherd and what He does for us.

Amen.

CHAPTER 11
JESUS, THE PRINCE OF LIFE

> *JOHN 11*
> *Verse 11*
> *These things said he: and after that he saith unto them, our friend Lazarus sleepeth; but I go, that I may awake him out of sleep (or Lazarus has fallen asleep – referring to his death.)*

Sleep.

The word sleep was often used by the writers to show the aftermath of life, as the body only sleeps.

DANIEL 12
Verse 2
And many of them that sleep in the dust of the earth shall awake, some to everlasting life, and some to shame and everlasting contempt.

The word death or falling asleep is shown in Stephen's case.

ACTS 7
Verse 60
And he kneeled down, and cried with a loud voice, Lord, lay not this sin to their charge. And when he had said this, he fell asleep.

Notice

When it talks of sleep in death, only the body is affected. The body was made of dust and therefore it will return to dust. The soul and spirit are not made of material substances as the body is, so they will not return to the dust. The body is now mortal. It will die and go back to the dust of the earth.

GENESIS 3
Verse 19
In the sweat of thy face shalt thou eat bread, till thou return unto the ground; for out of it wast thou taken: for dust thou art, and unto dust shalt thou return.

JAMES 2
Verse 26
For as the body without the spirit is dead, so faith without works is dead also.

This procedure will continue until sin is put down and death is destroyed.

I CORINTHIANS 15
Verse 26
The last enemy that shall be destroyed is death.

2 TIMOTHY 1
Verse 10
But is now made manifest by the appearing of our Saviour Jesus Christ, who hath <u>abolished death</u>, and hath brought life and immortality to light through the gospel:

In this verse alone there are four acts of Christ Jesus.
1. made manifest God's blessings by His bodily appearance on earth
2. He abolished death
3. He brought life through the gospel
4. He brought immortality through the gospel

I CORINTHIANS 15:55
O death, where is thy sting? O grave, where is thy victory?

HOSEA 13
Verse 14
I will ransom them from the power of the <u>grave</u>; I will redeem them from death: <u>O death, I will be thy plagues;</u> <u>O grave, I will be thy destruction</u>: repentance shall be hid from mine eyes.

REVELATION 1
Verse 18
I am he that liveth, and was dead; and, behold, I am alive for evermore, Amen; and have the keys of hell and of death.

As David wrote about sleeping in the dust, Jesus uses the figure of speech when He said, "The maid is not dead but sleepeth." Now He said the same about Lazarus, "Our friend sleepeth", denoting that only his body was sleeping.

Death only attacks the body making it lifeless until its resurrection at Christ's return. But remember, the person in that body does not sleep (or die) but lives with Him who is the resurrection and the life.

When Jesus rose again He ascended on High. He became the first fruits of those bodies whose bodies sleep (I Corinthians 15:20). When Christ returns, the spirit and soul of the bodies who now sleep, return with Him and will experience the redemption of the body.

With this universal conception of death, we now come to our Lords comforting words, "Our friend Lazarus sleepeth, but I go and awake him out of sleep." If Lazarus was only sleeping, there was no need of Jesus going to awake him. But this of which Jesus spoke was beyond the crises of sickness.

Peter, James and John were among them when He spoke of <u>death</u> or <u>sleep</u>. They should have remembered how He applied sleep in Matthew 9:24, "Give place for the maid is not <u>dead</u> but <u>sleepeth</u>."

Jesus then answered them, "Lazarus is dead."

> ### *Verse 4*
> *When Jesus heard that, he said, this sickness is not unto death, but for the glory of God, that the Son of God might be glorified thereby.*

This great story of Lazarus is a story of all mankind from creation until now. It takes one day for the messenger to reach Jesus and yet He tarries two more days and goes to the town of Bethany; the town of Mary and Martha. Let's see why it took four days to raise Lazarus. Let's notice something very special.

2 PETER 3
Verse 8
But, beloved, be not ignorant of this one thing, that one day is with the Lord as a thousand years, and a thousand years as one day.

From the creation until the translation of Enoch and the flood was 1000 years or one day. This refers from 4000 to 3000 years before Christ. This represents the first day Jesus gets the message about Lazarus. Now from the translation of Enoch to the covenant with Abraham was 1000 years or day two. This covenant made it possible for the Father to send Jesus to pay our debt of sin. We now have the day Jesus got the meassage and the second day that He tarried. This brings us to the next day He tarried, or the third day. From Abraham until the building of the Temple of Solomon was another 1000 years or day three.

Now from the building of the Temple of Solomon to the birth of Jesus was another 1000 years or one more day, day four.

Note: Day 1 – Message received (Creation to Enoch)
       Day 2 – Jesus tarried (Enoch unto Abraham)
       Day 3 – Jesus tarried (Abraham until Solomon's Temple)
       Day 4 – Comes to the tomb (Solomon's Temple until Christ)

His first coming was on the fourth day or 4000 years after Creation. Jesus waited two days in order to fulfill the Genesis Creation.

Notice a great truth about this fourth day...

GENESIS 1
Verse 14
And God said, let there be lights in the firmament of the heaven to divide the day from the night; and let them be for signs, and for seasons, and for days, and years:

Verse 19
And the evening and the morning were the fourth day.

Here on the fourth day of Creation, God brought the great light into creation. So, on this fourth day of the death of Lazarus we are about to see another great light given. In Genesis 3:9 God asks (concerning Adam), "Where art thou?" In John 11:34 Jesus asks (concerning Lazarus), "Where have you laid him?"

These two names have great meanings.
1. Lazarus – meaning "Life brought forth"
2. Adam – meaning "death or cast out"

The next great verse…

JOHN 11
Verse 35
Jesus wept.

The shortest verse in the Bible, yet it shows us so much about Christ. It was sowing the humanity of Jesus as the man Jesus (or the flesh). He wept with those who wept. Even His enemies noticed this.

Verse 36
Then said the Jews, Behold how he loved him!

They acknowledged His love and compassion for Lazarus.

Verse 37
And some of them said, Could not this man, which opened the eyes of the blind, have caused that even this man should not have died?

Remember verse 4? "This sickness is not unto death but for the Glory of God." They had no idea that a greater miracle was about to be performed than healing a blind man.

We now come to the tomb

Verse 38
Jesus therefore again groaning in himself cometh to the grave. It was a cave, and a stone lay upon it.

Verse 39
Jesus said, Take ye away the stone. Martha, the sister of him that was dead, saith unto him, Lord, by this time he stinketh: for he hath been dead four days.

When Jesus arrived on earth, mankind had been spiritually dead for 4000 years. Lazarus represents mankind. One day the message, yet He tarried two more days. Now on the fourth day Jesus is at the tomb. Now a great light is about to shine to redeem mankind.

Verse 43
*And when he thus had spoken, he cried with a loud voice, **Lazarus, come forth**.*

Compare

1. Genesis 1:3, "And God said let there be light, and there was light." Genesis 1:15b "…to give light upon the earth."
2. Jesus cried, "Come forth."

God's voice produced facts…
1. Light for men (1 above)
2. Light for man (2 above)

We now have two great miracles both on the fourth day, yet 4000 years apart.

We have shown the four days of Jesus at Lazarus' death and tomb. Now notice, Jesus said, "Take away the stone." This represents the fulfillment of the law.

MATTHEW 5
Verse 17

Think not that I am come to destroy the law, or the prophets: I am not come to destroy, but to fulfil.

When the Law had degenerated into legalism among the Pharisees, Jesus now takes the Law beyond outward observance to the inner spiritual intentions of God. The stone here represents the Law, for the Law had kept mankind entombed in spiritual death.

GALATIANS 3
Verse 23

But before faith came, we were kept under the law, shut up unto the faith which should afterwards be revealed.

Verse 24

Wherefore the law was our schoolmaster to bring us unto Christ, that we might be justified by faith.

The Law versus Grace

The Law Says	Grace Says
1.Keep off	Embrace him
2.Bow the knee	Kiss him
3.Punish him	Forgive him
4.Strip him	Put the best robe on him
5.Kills	Makes alive

When Christ made these statements, He opened up a whole new way.

The Way of Grace

G=God's
R=Riches
A=At
C=Christ's
E=Expense

Thus, the resurrection of Lazarus shows that we should be loosed from our bondages and customs and by lows of the religious world. The linen that Lazarus was wrapped in represented bondage and man-made laws, such as they couldn't eat with unwashed hands or couldn't walk through the fields eating corn on the Sabbath.

Notice

Loose him and let him go

JOHN 10
Verse 10
The thief cometh not, but for to steal, and to kill, and to destroy: I am come that they might have <u>life</u>, and that they might have it more abundantly.

We have shown you from the Garden of Eden until the covenant with Abraham, which was 2000 years and from Abraham until Christ, which was another 2000 years, thus showing the period from Eden to Christ as 4000 years or 4 days.

Remember, Lazarus' resurrection was for the Glory of God. Jesus said…

JOHN 11
Verse 25
Jesus said unto her, I am the resurrection, and the life: he that believeth in me, though he were dead, yet shall he live:

Thank God for the Prince of Life

<u>Amen.</u>

CHAPTER 12
JESUS, THE KING

JOHN 12
Verse 12
On the next day much people that were come to the feast, when they heard that Jesus was coming to Jerusalem,

Verse 13
Took branches of palm trees, and went forth to meet him, and cried, Hosanna: Blessed is the King of Israel that cometh in the name of the Lord.

Six days before Passover Jesus came to Bethany.

Bethany, meaning "a place of fruits.

Now we see Martha the practical soul and Mary the spiritual.

LUKE 10
Verse 40
But Martha was cumbered about much serving, and came to him, and said, Lord, dost thou not care that my sister hath left me to serve alone? Bid (*or tell*) her therefore that she help me.

Verse 41
And Jesus answered and said unto her, Martha, Martha, thou art careful (*or worried*) and troubled about many things:

Verse 42
But one thing is needful: and Mary hath chosen that good part, which shall not be taken away from her.

This can be explained in two ways. One, Jesus may be saying to Martha one dish would be sufficient. Two, Jesus could be saying one thing referring to the spiritual nourishment craved by Mary. In one sense Jesus may be implying that Martha should also leave her housework and concentrate on the urgent matter.

JOHN 12
Verse 3
Then took Mary a pound of ointment of spikenard, very costly, and anointed the feet of Jesus, and wiped his feet with her hair: and the house was filled with the odour of the ointment.

Mary, the devotional soul, was grateful for the awakening of her brother. When the soul is lifted up with thanksgiving and prayer, there follows an outflow of <u>love</u> that fills the whole house. The anointing of Jesus feet showed the willingness to serve. He said to His disciples, "He that is great among you, let him be your master.

MATTHEW 20
Verse 26
But it shall not be so among you: but whosoever will be great among you, let him be your minister;

I PETER 5
Verse 5[b]
...be clothed with humility

JOHN 12
Verse 7
Then said Jesus, Let her alone: against the day of my burying hath she kept this.

Notice

Jesus acknowledged the power of love when He said, "let her alone: against the day of my burying hath she done this." When personality is hurt (or put to death) and surrenders all, love pours her balm over every wound and the substance of her sympathy gives hope and faith.

JOHN 12
Verse 12
On the next day much people that were come to the feast, when they heard that Jesus was coming to Jerusalem,

Verse 13
Took branches of palm trees, and went forth to meet him, and cried, Hosanna: Blessed is the King of Israel that cometh in the name of the Lord.

Verse 14
And Jesus, when he had found a young ass, sat thereon; as it is written,

Verse 15
Fear not, daughter of Sion: behold, thy King cometh, sitting on an ass's colt.

Verse 20
And there were certain Greeks among them that came up to worship at the feast:

Verse 21
The same came therefore to Philip, which was of Bethsaida of Galilee, and desired (or asked) him, saying, Sir, we would see Jesus.

Verse 23
And Jesus answered them, saying, the hour is come, that the Son of man should be glorified.

Verse 24

Verily, verily, I say unto you, except a corn (or grain) of wheat fall into the ground and die, it abideth alone: but if it die, it bringeth forth much fruit.

In Verse 23, let's notice a few words that Jesus said...

The hour is come

The <u>hour is come</u> (<u>now</u>) for my <u>sufferings</u> and <u>glory</u> and the middle wall to be broken down between Jews and Gentiles so that they can be united into one body.

In Verses 20 and 21 we see why Jesus said this. There were Greeks among them at the feast (The same came to Philip <u>and saying we would see Jesus</u>.)

Now we must look at the statement "<u>the hour</u>".

JOHN 2
Verse 4
Jesus saith unto her, <u>Woman</u>, what have I to do with thee? <u>Mine hour is not yet come</u>.

In other words, my time for working miracles has not fully come. Jesus meant to wait until all the supply of wine was exhausted so that there would be <u>no doubt</u> about a miracle being performed.

Now...*Fill and Draw*

In the next text Jesus said, "My time is not yet come."

JOHN 7
Verse 3
His brethren therefore said unto him, Depart hence, and go into Judaea, that thy disciples also may see the works that thou doest.

Verse 4
For there is no man that doeth any thing in secret, and he himself seeketh to be known openly. If thou do these things, <u>shew thyself</u> to the world.

Verse 6
Then Jesus said unto them, <u>my time is not yet come</u>: but your time is alway ready.

Notice, Jesus is referring to His sufferings. If He made himself publicly known now it would only bring hate, for the world was looking for a <u>king.</u> Jesus had declined His <u>kingship</u>. The world could not believe this if He was the real <u>Messiah</u>.

JOHN 7
Verse 8
Go ye up unto this feast: I go not up yet unto this feast: <u>for my time is not yet full come</u>.

He wanted to be alone at this time for He went up later in secret. Could this be a figure of something else He was trying to show us?

Let's look at the Rapture. It will be done in secret as a thief in the night.

I THESSALONIANS
Verse 16
For the Lord, himself shall descend from heaven with a shout, with the voice of the archangel, and with the trump of God: and the dead in Christ shall rise first:

Verse 17
Then we which are alive and remain shall be caught up together with them in the clouds, to meet the Lord in the air: and so, shall we ever be with the Lord.

JOHN 7
Verse 10
But when his brethren were gone up, then went he also up unto the feast, not openly, but as it were in secret.

He who was seeking to save the lost was being in secret as to not be seen for worldly popularity and fame.

REVELATION 16
Verse 15
Behold, I come as a thief. Blessed is he that watcheth, and keepeth his garments, lest he walk naked, and they see his shame.

This is His announcement of His second coming and the battle of Armageddon.

REVELATION 16
Verse 16
And he gathered them together into a place called in the Hebrew tongue Armageddon.

Notice
In John 7, Verse 10, He came to the feast in secret. Then He showed himself openly, teaching in the temple.

JOHN 7
Verse 14
Now about the midst of the feast Jesus went up into the temple, and taught.

JOHN 7
Verse 30
Then they sought to take him: but no man laid hands on him, because his hour was not yet come.

JOHN 12
Verse 23
And Jesus answered them, saying, <u>the hour is come</u>, that the Son of man should be glorified.

Verse 24
Verily, verily, I say unto you, <u>except</u> a corn (or grain) of wheat fall into the ground and die, it abideth alone: but if it die, it bringeth forth much fruit.
Verily, verily, I say unto you, except a corn (or grain) of wheat fall into the ground and die, it abideth alone: but if it die, it bringeth forth much fruit.

Verse 27
Now is my soul troubled; and what shall I say? Father, <u>save me from this hour</u>: but for this cause came I unto this hour.

Now let's go back to John 12:23

Notice, in Verses 23-24, we see these things. Jesus compares himself as a grain of wheat. His <u>death</u> compared to a grain of wheat. His <u>resurrection</u> is the blade that springs up into everlasting life. His <u>manifestation</u> and <u>glorification</u> to the abundant fruit of the many grains produced to sustain life. <u>I must die to be fruitful</u>. I cannot establish a glorious church unless I am glorified.

EPHESIANS 1
Verse 5
Having predestinated (*or the foreknowledge of God*) us unto the adoption of children (*or as sons*) by Jesus Christ to himself, according to the good pleasure of his will.

ROMANS 8
Verse 29
For whom he did foreknow, he also did predestinate to be conformed to the image of his Son, that he might be the firstborn among many brethren.

The foreknowledge here should not be considered as getting acquainted with, but in the sense of bringing into a special relationship with God.

AMOS 3
Verse 2[a]
You only <u>have I known</u> of all the families of the earth:

This means in the sense of God setting Israel apart to bring her into a covenant relationship with Himself. Now let us see something very special about the death and why we must follow His example.

MARK 8
Verse 34
And when he had called the people unto him with his disciples also, he said unto them, whosoever will come after me, let him <u>deny himself</u>, and <u>take up his cross</u>, and follow me.

The gospel benefits are solely on the basis of personal choice and <u>meeting certain conditions.</u> There are four things one must do after being saved (or born again).
1. Continue following Jesus (Mark 7:24)
2. Deny himself – removing all self-dependence and self interests which are contrary to God (Romans 6:16)
3. Take up the cross daily (Romans 6:11-13)
4. Follow Christ daily, not for a little while (John 10:26-28)

These three things one must do and continue to do to have eternal life.
1. Believe – which implies complete and continued obedience (John 10:26)
2. Ear His voice – be not hearers only but also doers of His word (James 1:22)
3. Follow Christ – not only at the beginning of a Christian experience, but daily and throughout life (Luke 9:23)

To take up our cross and follow Christ, we must bear fruit. Let's look in Romans.

ROMANS 5
Verse 21
That as sin hath reigned unto death, even so might grace reign through righteousness unto eternal life by Jesus Christ our Lord.

ROMANS 6
Verse 1
What shall we say then? Shall we continue in sin, that grace may abound?
Verse 2
<u>God forbid</u>. How shall we, that are <u>dead to sin</u>, live any longer therein?

Reasons not to live in sin...
1. Death to sin (Romans 6:1-2)
2. Resurrection from spiritual death (Romans 6:4-5)
3. Walk in newness of life (Romans 6:4)
4. Death to sin and resurrection from sin means <u>walking like</u> Christ (Romans 6:5)
5. The old man is crucified (Romans 6:6)
6. The body of sin is destroyed (Romans 6:6)
7. Freed from sin (Romans 6:7)
8. Faith counts <u>sin</u> dead (Romans 6:8)
9. Sin has no dominion over us (Romans 6:9)
10. Sin shall not reign in our body (Romans 6:12)
11. Body must not yield to sin (Romans 6:13)
12. Married to Christ (Romans 7:4)
13. Walk in the Spirit (Romans 8:1- dead (Romans 6:8)

14. Made free from the law of sin (Romans 8:2)
15. To be spiritually minded (Romans 8:6)
16. Christ in us not sin (Romans 8:10)
17. We are not debtors to sin (Romans 8:12)
18. Spirit mortifies sin in us (Romans 8:13)
19. We have the Spirit of freedom (Romans 8:15)
20. Intercession of Christ and the Holy Spirit keeps us (Romans 8:26-27 & 34)

By these 20 reasons for not being in sin and we're baptized into Christ, not water baptism (John 3:5-6). Born of water – natural birth. Born of Spirit – spiritual birth. So, we are baptized into His death. We should walk in the newness of life.

These are the fruits of the Spirit when we die to self. In Verse 6 we are crucified with Him that henceforth we should not serve sin (Galatians 5:22) …But the fruit of the Spirit is
1. Love (I Corinthians 13:4)
2. Joy (Matthew 21:9)
3. Peace (Isaiah 45:7)
4. Longsuffering (I Corinthians 13:4 & 7)
5. Gentleness (2 Timothy 2:24-26)
6. Goodness (Romans 2:4)
7. Faith (Hebrews 10:19-23 & 11:1)
8. Meekness (Psalms 25:9)
9. Temperance (Romans 13:14)

…against such there is no law.

Are you crucified with Christ?

CHAPTER 13
JESUS, THE SERVANT

> ### JOHN 13
> ### Verse 16
> *Verily, verily, I say unto you, the <u>servant</u> is not greater than his lord; neither he that is sent greater than he that sent him.*

Servant – meaning "one who serves others".

John here in this chapter does not give what took place before supper. All accounts were directed the meal of the Passover, and the common center of interest was the last meal with His disciples. Jesus knew the identity of the one who was to betray him. The part after the foot-washing comes into light when we put it together with another scripture, as foot-washing is a mere example of <u>humility of a servant.</u>

LUKE 22
Verse 24
And there was also a <u>strife among them</u>, which of them should be accounted the greatest.

Verse 25
And he said unto them, the kings of the Gentiles exercise lordship over them; and they that exercise authority upon them are called benefactors.

Verse 26
But <u>ye shall not be so</u>: but he that is greatest among you, let him be as the younger; and he that is chief, <u>as he that doth serve</u>.

Verse 27
For whether is greater, he that sitteth at meat, or he that serveth? is not he that sitteth at meat? <u>but I am among you as he that serveth</u>.

Notice, what Jesus is saying here is the standard of greatness is to be served. <u>God's is to serve.</u>

1. Man's standard is to be served (or receives)
2. God's standard is to give
3. Man's standard is to <u>humble others</u>
4. God's standard is to <u>humble one's self</u>

Failure to Obey...Disobedience Brought...

ISAIAH 14
Verse 12
How art thou fallen from heaven, O Lucifer, son of the morning! How art thou cut down to the ground, which didst weaken the nations!

Greatness or disobedience caused him to be cast out.

GENESIS 3
Verse 11
And he said, who told thee that thou wast naked? Hast thou eaten of the tree, whereof I commanded thee that thou shouldest not eat?

Their disobedience to God to become as Him caused them <u>to be cast out of Eden.</u>

GENESIS 3
Verse 24
So, he drove out the man; and he placed at the east of the garden of Eden Cherubims, and a flaming sword which turned every way, to keep the way of <u>the tree of life</u>.

Disobedience caused Adam to fall and then be cast out of the Garden of Eden. "Drove out" means he lost his possession or dominion of Earth.

LUKE 22
Verse 27
For whether is <u>greater</u>, he that <u>sitteth</u> at meat, or he that <u>serveth</u>? is not he that sitteth at meat? but <u>I am among you</u> as he that serveth.

Verse 28
Ye are they which have continued with me in my temptations.

In essence, He was saying to them, "You are supposed to be with me in my trials and here you are discussing who is greatest in the Kingdom."

MARK 10
Verse 37
They said unto him, Grant unto us that we may sit, one on thy right hand, and the other on thy left hand, in thy glory.

Verse 41
And when <u>the ten</u> heard it, they began to be much displeased with James and John.

Notice, now we see why Jesus, after supper, became a servant to His disciples.

John 13
Verse 16
And when the ten heard it, they began to be much displeased with James and John.

MATTHEW 18
Verse 4
Whosoever therefore shall <u>humble himself</u> as this little child, the same is greatest in the kingdom of heaven.

The way of <u>greatness</u> in the world is to go up by any way you can, even at the expense of others. The way of the <u>Gospel</u> is to go down to become the least, considering the other brother the better man.

ROMANS 12
Verse 10
Be kindly affectioned one to another with brotherly love; in honour preferring one another;

John 13
Verse 4
He riseth from supper, and laid aside his garments; and took a towel, and girded himself.

Verse 5
After that he poureth water into a bason, and <u>began to wash the disciples' feet</u>, and to wipe them with the towel wherewith he was girded.

Jesus, after the supper was finished, began to wash the disciples' feet. The reason for this example was not so much as an example of foot-washing but to show forgiveness and love for His disciples, even though one would betray Him (Judas Iscariot). We believe that Jesus was trying to show that we should become as little children. Little children argue and have dissention among themselves but are quick to forgive. The ten disciples no doubt were still in much contention of what James and John asked Jesus.

Now Jesus was about to teach them one more time about contentions among them. He showed them that whosoever would be great among them should be their servant. The Son of Man came to minister and to give His life a ransom for all. To have everything for one's self is to be as a child, but to do for others is to reach manhood.

I CORINTHIANS 13
Verse 11
When I was a <u>child</u>, I <u>spake</u> as a <u>child</u>, I <u>understood</u> as a <u>child</u>, I <u>thought</u> as a <u>child</u>: but when I became a <u>man</u>, I put away childish things.

There is more important things than to have discord at the last supper in which Jesus was eating with them, as the <u>hour had now come</u> for His betrayal.
Jesus shows His great love as a servant, for His disciples, even Judas. For He also washed Judas's feet. After washing all of their feet, He came to Peter.

Peter saith, "Doest thou wash my feet?" In Verse 8, Peter saith unto Him, "Thou shalt <u>never</u> wash my feet." Notice, pride takes over. He felt it was below his dignity to wash his feet.
Jesus rebuked him very subtly, "If I wash thee not, thou hast no part with Me."
In Verse 9 we see a different Peter, for he said, "Lord not my feet only but also my hands and my head."

Notice

Peter, I believe, took this as a spiritual washing and wanted to be clean.

John 13
Verse 10
Jesus saith to him, He that is washed needeth not save to wash his feet, but is <u>clean</u> every whit: and ye are clean, <u>but not all</u>.

Verse 11
For he knew who should betray him; therefore, said he, Ye are not all clean.

Clean means "pure and innocent"

John 13

Verse 12

So, <u>after</u> he had washed their feet, and had taken his garments, and was set down again, he said unto them, <u>Know ye what I have done to you?</u>

Verse 14

If I then, your <u>Lord</u> and <u>Master</u>, have washed your feet; <u>ye also ought to wash one another's feet.</u>

Verse 15

For I have given you <u>an example</u>, that ye should do as I have done to you.

PHILIPPIANS 2
Verse 7

But made himself of no reputation, and took upon him the form of a <u>servant</u>, and was made in the likeness of men:

Verse 8

And being found in fashion as a man, <u>he humbled himself, and became obedient</u> unto death, even the death of the cross.

Notice, Christ humbled Himself from a divine form to a human form and from sinless humanity to become sin for us, even the death on the cross.

John 13

Verse 17

If ye know these things, happy are ye if ye do them.

Verse 17 is not necessarily referring to feet-washing but services to others who are in need and those who are the least in the world.

REVELATION 16
Verse 15

Behold, I come <u>as a thief</u>. <u>Blessed</u> is he that <u>watcheth</u>, and <u>keepeth</u> his garments, lest he walk naked, and they see his shame.

CHAPTER 14
JESUS, THE COUNSELOR

JOHN 14
Verse 1
Let not your heart be troubled: ye believe in God, <u>believe also in me.</u>

Verse 2
In my Father's house <u>are many mansions</u>: if it were not so, I would have told you. I go to prepare a place for you.

Verse 3
And if I go and prepare a place for you, <u>I will come again</u>, and <u>receive you unto myself</u>; that where I am, <u>there</u> ye may be also.

There are some great truths after the Passover supper in the 14th chapter of John. After supper, they sang a hymn.

MARK 14
Verse 26
And when they had sung an hymn, they went out into the mount of Olives.

MATTHEW 26
Verse 30
And when they had sung an hymn, they went out into the mount of Olives.

Here are some of the Psalms He may have sung.

PSALMS 113
Verse 2
Blessed be the name of the LORD from this time forth and for evermore.

PSALMS 114
Verse 1
When Israel went out of Egypt, the house of Jacob from a people of strange language;

PSALMS 115
Verse 1
Not unto us, O LORD, not unto us, but unto thy name give glory, for thy mercy, and for thy truth's sake.

Verse 12
The LORD hath been mindful of us: he will bless us; he will bless the house of Israel; he will bless the house of Aaron.

PSALMS 116
Verse 3
The sorrows of death compassed me, and the <u>pains of hell</u> gat hold upon me: I found trouble and sorrow.

PSALMS 117
Verse 2
For his merciful kindness is great toward us: and the truth of the LORD endureth for ever. Praise ye the LORD.

PSALMS 118
Verse 1
O give thanks unto the LORD; for he is good: <u>because</u> his mercy endureth for ever.

These Psalms from 113 to 118 all speak about His future happiness from the upper room to His ascension and then to His return. Let's notice His last sermon there in the upper room.

John 14, Verse 1...

1. He speaks about Heaven:
   a. His father has many abodes
   b. He is going there to prepare a place
   c. Concerning His return

   (Please note, Verse 1, "I go and prepare a place, and if I go, I will come again." This is the only place in the four gospels (Matthew, Mark, Luke & John) where this is mentioned about the rapture where God promised to come back to take His people off the earth.)

2. He is questioned by Philip and Thomas:
   a. Thomas – "How can we know the way?" Jesus – "I am the way the truth and the life."
   b. Philip – "Show us the father." Jesus – He who hath seen me hath seen the father."

3. He speaks of the Holy Spirit:
   a. The Holy Spirit will come and dwell with them forever.
   b. The Holy Spirit will come and teach them all things.

4. He is questioned by Judas (<u>not Iscariot</u>):
   a. Judas – "How will you manifest yourself to us and not to the world?" Jesus – If anyone loves me he will keep my word." "My father will love him and <u>we</u> will come to him and make our abode with him."

5. He speaks about peace.
    a. He promised to leave peace with them.
    b. The peace would keep their hearts from trouble and fear.

The Continuation of His Sermon

The Savior

(Christ Himself)

1. The mystery of His Return:
    a. **John 14:3** - And if I go and prepare a place for you, I will come again, and receive you unto myself; that where I am, there ye may be also.

2. The mystery of His body:
    a. **John 14:20** - At that day ye shall know that I am in my Father, and ye in me, and I in you.
    b. **Ephesians 3:1-7** – 1) For this cause I Paul, the prisoner of Jesus Christ for you Gentiles, 2) If ye have heard of the dispensation of the grace of God which is given me to you-ward: 3) How that by revelation he made known unto me the mystery; (as I wrote afore in few words, 4) Whereby, when ye read, ye may understand my knowledge in the mystery of Christ) 5) which in other ages was not made known unto the sons of men, as it is now revealed unto his holy apostles and prophets by the Spirit; 6) That the gentiles should be fellow heirs, and of the same body, and partakers of his promise in Christ by the gospel: 7) Whereof I was made a minister, according to the gift of the grace of God given unto me by the effectual working of his power.
    c. **Colossians 1:24-27** – 1) Who now rejoice in my sufferings for you, and fill up that which is behind of the afflictions of Christ in my flesh for his body's sake, which is the church: 25) Where of I am made a minister, according to the dispensation of God which is given to me for you, to fulfil the word of God; 26) Even the mystery which hath been hid from ages and from generations, but now is made manifest to his saints: 27) To whom God would make known what is the riches of the glory of this mystery among the Gentiles; which is Christ in you, the hope of glory:

(Christ and His Father)

1. He declares Him:
    a. **John 14:7-9** – 7) If ye had known me, ye should have known my Father also: and from henceforth ye know him, and have seen him. 8) Philip saith unto him, Lord, show us the Father, and it sufficeth us. 9) Jesus saith unto him, have I been so long time with you, and yet hast thou not known me, Philip? He that hath seen me hath seen the Father; and how sayest thou then, Show us the Father?

2. He is inseparable from Him; linked to Him:
    a. **John 14:10-11** – 10) Believest thou not that I am in the Father, and the Father in me? The words that I speak unto you I speak not of myself: but the Father that dwelleth in me, he doeth the works. 11) Believe me that I am in the Father, and the Father in me: or else believe me for the very works' sake.

3. He glorifies Him:
   a. **John 14:13** – And whatsoever ye shall ask in my name, that will I do, that the Father may be glorified in the Son.

4. He goes to Him:
   a. **John 14:2** – In my Father's house are many mansions: if it were not so, I would have told you. I go to prepare a place for you.
   b. **John 14:12** – Verily, verily, I say unto you, He that believeth on me, the works that I do shall he do also; and greater works than these shall he do; because I go unto my Father.
   c. **John 14:28** – Ye have heard how I said unto you, I go away, and come again unto you. If ye loved me, ye would rejoice, because I said, I go unto the Father: for my Father is greater than I.
   d. **John 16:10** – Ye have heard how I said unto you, I go away, and come again unto you. If ye loved me, ye would rejoice, because I said, I go unto the Father: for my Father is greater than I.
   e. **John 16:**28 – I came forth from the Father, and am come into the world: again, I leave the world, and go to the Father.

(Christ and the Holy Spirit)

1. He comes at Christ's prayer:
   a. **John 14:16** – And I will pray the Father, and he shall give you another Comforter, that he may abide with you for ever;

2. He comes to honor and testify concerning Him:
   a. **John 15:26** – But when the Comforter is come, whom I will send unto you from the Father, even the Spirit of truth, which proceedeth from the Father, he shall testify of me:
   b. **John 16:13-15** – 13) Howbeit when he, the Spirit of truth, is come, he will guide you into all truth: for he shall not speak of himself; but whatsoever he shall hear, that shall he speak: and he will shew you things to come. 14) He shall glorify me: for he shall receive of mine, and shall shew it unto you. 15) All things that the Father hath are mine: therefore, said I, that he shall take of mine, and shall shew it unto you.
   c. **John 16:7-11** – 7) Nevertheless I tell you the truth; it is expedient for you that I go away: for if I go not away, the Comforter will not come unto you; but if I depart, I will send him unto you. 8) And when he is come, he will reprove the world of sin, and of righteousness, and of judgment: 9) of sin, because they believe not on me; 10) of righteousness, because I go to my Father, and ye see me no more; 11) of judgment, because the prince of this world is judged.

(Christ and the Believer)

1. He is the vine:
   a. **John 15:1-8** – 1) I am the true vine, and my Father is the husbandman. 2) Every branch in me that beareth not fruit he taketh away: and every branch that beareth fruit, he purgeth it, that it may bring forth more fruit. 3) Now ye are clean through the word which I have spoken unto you. 4) Abide in me, and I in you. As the branch cannot bear fruit of itself, except it abide in the vine; no more can ye, except ye abide in me. 5) I am the vine, ye are the branches: He that abideth in me, and I in him, the same bringeth forth much fruit: for without me ye can do nothing. 6) If a man

abide not in me, he is cast forth as a branch, and is withered; and men gather them, and cast them into the fire, and they are burned. 7) If ye abide in me, and my words abide in you, ye shall ask what ye will, and it shall be done unto you. 8) Herein is my Father glorified, that ye bear much fruit; so shall ye be my disciples.

    b. **John 15:16** - Ye have not chosen me, but I have chosen you, and ordained you, that ye should go and bring forth fruit, and that your fruit should remain: that whatsoever ye shall ask of the Father in my name, he may give it you.

2. They are the branches:
   a. **John 15:5** - I am the vine, ye are the branches: He that abideth in me, and I in him, the same bringeth forth much fruit: for without me ye can do nothing.

Now…

The Saint or Believer

(The Believer and the Father)

1. Indwelled by the Father:
   a. **John 14:23** – Jesus answered and said unto him, if a man love me, he will keep my words: and my Father will love him, and we will come unto him, and make our abode with him.

2. Loved by the Father:
   a. **John 14:21** – He that hath my commandments, and keepeth them, he it is that loveth me: and he that loveth me shall be loved of my Father, and I will love him, and will manifest myself to him.
   b. **John 16:27** – For the Father himself loveth you, because ye have loved me, and have believed that I came out from God.

3. Empowered to do great works:
   c. **John 14:12** – Verily, verily, I say unto you, He that believeth on me, the works that I do shall he do also; and greater works than these shall he do; because I go unto my Father.

(The Believer and the Holy Spirit)

1. To teach believers all things:
   a. **John 14:26** – But the Comforter, which is the Holy Ghost, whom the Father will send in my name, he shall teach you all things, and bring all things to your remembrance, whatsoever I have said unto you.
   b. **John 16:14-15** – 14) He shall glorify me: for he shall receive of mine, and shall shew it unto you. 15) All things that the Father hath are mine: therefore, said I, that he shall take of mine, and shall shew it unto you.

2. To abide forever:
   a. **John 14:16** – And I will pray the Father, and he shall give you another Comforter, that he may abide with you for ever;

(The Believer and Persecution)

1. To expect many persecutions:
   a. **John 14:17** – Even the Spirit of truth; whom the world cannot receive, because it seeth him not, neither knoweth him: but ye know him; for he dwelleth with you, and shall be in you.
   b. **John 15:18-21** – 18) If the world hate you, ye know that it hated me before it hated you. 19) If ye were of the world, the world would love his own: but because ye are not of the world, but I have chosen you out of the world, therefore the world hateth you. 20) remember the word that I said unto you, the servant is not greater than his lord. If they have persecuted me, they will also persecute you; if they have kept my saying, they will keep yours also. 21) But all these things will they do unto you for my name's sake, because they know not him that sent me.

2. To rejoice in persecutions:
   a. **John 16:1-4** – 1) These things have I spoken unto you, that ye should not be offended. 2) They shall put you out of the synagogues: yea, the time cometh, that whosoever killeth you will think that he doeth God service. 3) And these things will they do unto you, because they have not known the Father, nor me. 4)
   b. **John 16:20-22** – 20) verily, verily, I say unto you, that ye shall weep and lament, but the world shall rejoice: and ye shall be sorrowful, but your sorrow shall be turned into joy. 21) A woman when she is in travail hath sorrow, because her hour is come: but as soon as she is delivered of the child, she remembereth no more the anguish, for joy that a man is born into the world. 22) And ye now therefore have sorrow: but I will see you again, and your heart shall rejoice, and your joy no man taketh from you.
   c. **John 16:33** – These things I have spoken unto you, that in me ye might have peace. In the world ye shall have tribulation: but be of good cheer; I have overcome the world.

(The Believer and other Believers)

1. To love them:
   a. **John 15:12-14** – 12) this is my commandment, that ye love one another, as I have loved you. 13) Greater love hath no man than this that a man lay down his life for his friends. 14) Ye are my friends, if ye do whatsoever I command you.
   b. **John 15:17** – These things I command you, that ye love one another.

PSALMS 118
Verse 26
Blessed be he that cometh in the name of the LORD: we have blessed you out of the house of the LORD.

Note, He said "I go away and I will come again.

I JOHN 3
Verse 2

Beloved, now are we the sons of God, and it doth not yet appear what we shall be: <u>but we know</u> <u>that</u>, when he shall appear, we shall be like him; for we shall see him as he is.

> ### John 14
> ### Verse 27
> *Peace I leave with you, my peace I give unto you: not as the world giveth, give I unto you. Let not your heart be troubled, neither let it be afraid.*

<u>Notice Jesus</u>

I leave you my last, my best, my dying peace. Not the kind the world gives you, but everlasting peace.

Thank God for this Chapter. The greatest thing about it is
"<u>I will come again!</u>"

<u>Amen!</u>

CHAPTER 15
JESUS, THE TRUE VINE

> ### *JOHN 15*
> ### *Verse 1*
> *I am the true vine, and my Father is the husbandman.*
>
> ### *Verse 2*
> *Every branch <u>in me</u> that beareth not fruit <u>he taketh away</u>: and every branch that beareth fruit, <u>he purgeth it</u>, that it may bring forth more fruit.*

Notice, if the believer is fruitful, he is purged.

Purge means "to cleanse thoroughly." To produce more fruit, if he is fruitless, he is taken away or removed from being part of the branches. The father or husbandman does this.

JOHN 10
Verse 29
My Father, which gave them me, is greater than all; and no man is able to pluck them out of my Father's hand.

John 15
Verse 4
Abide in me, and I in you. As the branch cannot bear fruit of itself, except it abide in the vine; no more can ye, except ye abide in me.

Notice…except you abide in Him… unless you become one as in marriage, as Adam and Eve became one to bring forth fruit before Satan entered into them. They were cut off.

This means to be of one mind and one spirit being in Christ.

ROMANS 8
Verse 4
That the righteousness of the law might be fulfilled in us, who walk not after the flesh, but after the Spirit.

Verse 7
Because the carnal mind is enmity (*or active mutual* hatred) against God: for it is not subject to the law of God, neither indeed can be.

To set your affections on the sins of the flesh.

GALATIANS 5
Verse 16
This I say then, Walk in the Spirit, and ye shall not fulfil the lust of the flesh.

Verse 17
For the flesh lusteth against the Spirit, and the Spirit against the flesh: and these are contrary the one to the other: so that ye cannot do the things that ye would.

ROMANS 6
Verse 19
I speak after the manner of men because of the infirmity of your flesh: for as ye have yielded your members servants to uncleanness and to iniquity unto iniquity; even so now yield your members servants to righteousness unto holiness.

ROMANS 8
Verse 8
So, then they that are in the flesh cannot please God.

Minding the sins of the flesh is enmity towards God.

Enmity – Active mutual hatred.

ROMANS 8
Verse 7
Because the carnal mind is enmity against God: for it is not subject to the law of God, neither indeed can be.

JAMES 1
Verse 14
But every man is tempted, <u>when</u> he is drawn away of his own lust, and enticed.

There are seven steps to temptations in this chapter:

1. Tempted – (Verse 14)
2. Drawn away – strong imaginations (Verse 14)
3. Lust – delight in viewing it – (Verse 14)
4. Enticed – weakening of one's will (verse 15)
5. Lust conceived – yielding (Verse 15)
6. Sin – Sinful act committed (Verse 15)
7. Death – result of actual sin (Verse 15)

JAMES 4
Verse 4
Ye adulterers and adulteresses, <u>know ye not</u> that the friendship of the world is enmity with God? Whosoever therefore will be a friend of the world is the enemy of God.

The believer and the world...

<u>He must...</u>

1. Be free from cares (Matthew 13:22)
2. Not gain the world at the expense of his soul (Matthew 16:26)
3. Not offend others (Matthew 18:7)
4. Not be of the world (John 15:19)
5. Not love his life in the world (John 12:25)
6. Be delivered from the world (James 1:4)
7. Be crucified to the world (Galatians 6:14)
8. Shine as a light to the world (Philippians 2:15)
9. Deny it's (the world's) lusts and live godly in it (Titus 2:12)
10. Be unspotted from the world (James 1:27)
11. Not be friends of the world (James 4:4)
12. Escape the corruption of the world (II Peter 1:4)
13. Love not the world or things in the world (I John 2:15-17)

14. Be like Christ in the world (I John 4:17)

15. Overcome the world (I John 5:4-5_
16. Be chosen out (John 15:19)
17. Be not conformed to it (Romans 12:2)
18. Be dead to its ways (Colossians 2:20)

John 15
Verse 5
I am the vine, ye are the branches: He that abideth in me, and I in him, the same bringeth forth much fruit: for without <u>me</u> ye can do nothing.

Verse 6
If a man abide not in me, he is cast forth as a branch, and is withered; and men gather them, and cast them into the fire, and they are burned.

The words "abide" or "abideth" appear ten times in the first ten verses of John 15.

Verse 7
If ye abide in me, and my words abide in you, ye shall ask <u>what ye will</u>, and <u>it shall be done</u> unto you.

Verse 8
Herein is my Father glorified, that ye bear much fruit; so shall ye be my disciples.

Let's note some great lessons in John 15:1-8...

1. God is the Husbandman (Verse 1)
2. Christ is the vine (Verses 1-5)
3. Believers are the branches (Verses 2 & 5)
4. Every fruitless branch is cut off (Verses 2 & 6)
5. Every fruitless branch is purged (Verses 2 & 5)
6. Every branch is clean (Verse 3)
7. Branches <u>must</u> abide in Christ (Verses 4 & 5)
8. The branch is helpless by itself (Verses 4 & 5)
9. The branch remains in Him to bear fruit (verses 4 & 6)
10. The branch must abide in Christ or be cut off (Verse 6)
11. The branches must have His words abiding (Verse 7)
12. The branches must glorify Christ to bring forth much fruit (Verse 8)

ISAIAH 5
(The Song of God's Vineyard)

Verse 1
Now will I sing to my wellbeloved a song of my beloved touching his vineyard? My wellbeloved hath a vineyard in a very fruitful hill:

Verse 2
And he fenced it, and gathered out the stones thereof, and planted it with the choicest vine, and built a tower in the midst of it, and also made a winepress therein: and he looked that it should bring forth grapes, and it brought forth wild grapes.

Let's note these verses...

1. Jehovah has a vineyard (Verse 1)
2. On a fruitful hill (Verse 1)
3. He fenced it (Verse 2)
4. He gathered out the stones (Verse 2)
5. He planted the choicest vines (Verse 2)
6. He built a tower in the midst (Verse 2)
7. He made a winepress in it (Verse 2)
8. He expected good grapes (Verse 2)
9. He harvested wild grapes (Verse 2)

Notice...

John 15
Verse 5
I am the vine, ye *are* the branches: He that abideth in me, and I in him, the same bringeth forth much fruit: for without me ye can do nothing.

Verse 8
Herein is my Father glorified, that ye bear much fruit; so, shall ye be my disciples.

Let's see what the husbandman did in **Isaiah 5**.

ISAIAH 5
Verse 3
And now, O inhabitants of Jerusalem, and men of Judah, judge, I pray you, betwixt me and my vineyard.

Verse 4
What could have been done more to my vineyard that I have not done in it? Wherefore, when I looked that it should bring forth grapes, brought it forth wild grapes?

Verse 5

And now go to; I will tell you what I will do to my vineyard: I will take away the hedge thereof, and it shall be eaten up; and break down the wall thereof, and it shall be trodden down:

Verse 6

And I will lay it waste: it shall not be pruned, nor digged; but there shall come up briers and thorns: I will also command the clouds that they rain no rain upon it.

Notice, when the husbandman set judgment on His vineyard...the husbandman said,

1. I will take away the hedge (Verse 5)
2. The vineyard shall be eaten up (Verse 5)
3. The walls would be broken down (Verse 5)
4. The vineyard would be trodden down (Verse 5)
5. The vineyard would lay a waste (Verse 6)
6. The husbandman would not prune it (Verse 6)
7. The husbandman would not dig or cultivate it (Verse 6)
8. That it should bear briers and thorns (Verse 6)
9. The there would be no rain on it (Verse 6)

Verse 5

I am the vine, ye are the branches: He that abideth in me, and I in him, the same bringeth forth much fruit: for without me ye can do nothing.

Verse 8

Herein is my Father glorified, that ye bear much fruit; so, shall ye be my disciples.

CHAPTER 16
JESUS, THE GIVER OF THE HOLY SPIRIT

JOHN 16
Verse 7

Nevertheless, I tell you the truth; It is expedient for you that I go away: for if I go not away, the Comforter (or advocate) will not come unto you; but if I depart, I will send him to you.

JOHN 14
Verse 26

But the Comforter, which is the Holy Ghost, whom the Father will send in my name, he shall teach you all things, and bring all things to your remembrance, whatsoever I have said unto you.

Notice here in these verses we see the Comforter as one who is call of God to be a help or Council.

I JOHN 2
Verse 1
My little children, these things write I unto you, that ye sin not. And if any man sin, we have an <u>advocate</u> with the Father, Jesus Christ the righteous:

Note – the word "Advocate" means "a helper" The Holy Spirit is our <u>Paraclete or helper</u> here on earth, while <u>Jesus</u> is our <u>paraclete or helper</u> in Heaven.

John 16
Verse 8
And when <u>he is come</u>, he will reprove the world of sin, and of righteousness, and of judgment:

Verse 9
<u>Of sin</u>, because they believe not on me;

Verse 10
<u>Of righteousness</u>, because I go to my Father, and ye see me no more;

Verse 11
<u>Of judgment</u>, because the prince of this world is judged.

Verse 13
Howbeit <u>when</u> he, the Spirit of truth, is come, <u>he will guide you into all truth:</u> for he shall <u>not speak of himself;</u> but <u>whatsoever he shall hear, that shall he speak: and he will shew you things to come.</u>

In these verses, we see some great truths.

1. Reprove – convict
2. The world – all men
3. Sin – unbelief or the foundation for sin
4. Righteousness – that man's righteousness is useless
5. Judgment – men who believe in Christ will escape the eternal damnation (and) those who refuse to believe will be eternally damned.

Now let's notice…

JOHN 16
Verse 13[a]
Howbeit when he, the Spirit of truth, is come…

JOHN 20
Verse 22
And when he had said this, he <u>breathed on them</u>, and saith unto them, Receive ye the Holy Ghost:

Verse 23
Whose soever sins ye remit (*or forgive*), they are remitted (*or forgiven*) unto them; and whose soever sins ye retain (*or use strength*), they are retained (*or take dominion over*). (Strong's #2902 and Strong's 2904)

There is another form of expressing God's power to bind or loose things on earth.

MATTHEW 18
Verse 18
Verily I say unto you, <u>whatsoever</u> ye shall bind on earth shall be bound in heaven: and whatsoever ye shall loose on earth shall be loosed in heaven.

MATTHEW 16
Verse 19
And I will give unto thee <u>the keys</u> of the kingdom of heaven: and whatsoever thou shalt bind on earth shall be bound in heaven: and whatsoever thou shalt loose on earth shall be loosed in heaven.

The word <u>Keys</u> here represents power or authority.

ISAIAH 22
Verse 22
And the key of the house of David will I lay upon his shoulder; so, he shall open, and none shall shut; and he shall shut, and none shall open.

The key carried on the shoulder showed evidence of property or trust an emblem of authority. Thus, the binding and loosening means more than declaring something lawful or unlawful by preaching, it means to <u>confirm the truth</u> by power as <u>Christ</u> and the apostles did. This is why Jesus made this statement in the Book of Acts.

ACTS 1
Verse 8
But <u>ye shall receive power, after that</u> the Holy Ghost is come <u>upon</u> you: and <u>ye shall</u> be witnesses unto me both in Jerusalem, and in all Judaea, and in Samaria, and <u>unto</u> the uttermost parts of the earth.

I PETER
Verse 3
Blessed be the God and Father of our Lord Jesus Christ, which according to his abundant mercy <u>hath</u> begotten us <u>again</u> unto a lively hope by the resurrection of Jesus Christ from the dead,

Verse 4
To an inheritance (*or possession*) incorruptible (*or immortal*), and undefiled (*Holy*), and that fadeth not away (*or unfading*), reserved (*or guarded against* loss) in heaven for you,

Notice, He was Holy; He was harmless; He was undefiled; He was separate from sinners; He lived a perfect life not being unequally yoked together with sinners in their sinful ways; he was separate; he was made higher than the heavens; He was exalted more than any other angels or created beings of Heaven.

I PETER 1
Verse 10
Of which salvation the prophets have enquired and searched diligently, who prophesied of the grace that should come unto you?

They carefully and diligently sought the truth of all things that they were prophesying. They examined the salvation, grace and the gifts of the Spirit. It was the fullness of grace they predicted.

JOHN 1
Verse 16
And of his fulness have all we received, and grace for grace.

Verse 17
For the law was given by Moses, but grace and truth came by Jesus Christ.

ACTS 2
Verse 1
And when the day of Pentecost was fully come, they were all with one accord in one place.

Verse 2
And suddenly there came a sound from heaven as of a rushing mighty wind, and it filled all the house where they were sitting.

The sound that preceded the actual filling of the Spirit was a sound to get the attention of each member of those in the upper room; a sound they would never forget. This sound was an outward sign of the descent of a Divine person, the Holy Spirit, who would come to dwell in the believers to form the body of Christ.

EPHESIANS 2
Verse 18
For through him we both have access by one Spirit unto the father.

Verse 19
Now therefore ye are no more strangers and foreigners, but fellow citizens with the saints, and of the household of God;

As we see Pentecost approaching, we notice that they went into the upper room one hundred and twenty, and after the wind blew they became as one (in one accord). They were citizens of equal rights with one another and of all who became part of God's household.

JOHN 3
Verse 8
The wind bloweth where it listeth (*or wishes*), and thou hearest the sound thereof, but canst not tell whence it cometh, and whither it goeth: so is every one that is born of the Spirit.

PSALMS 104
Verse 4
Who maketh his spirits angels; his ministers (*or servants*) a flaming fire?

The scripture notes that there was a sound <u>as of</u> a <u>rushing mighty wind</u>. There was a sound <u>as of a mighty</u> <u>wind</u>, but all was still. The disciples had seen many wind storms before on the Sea of Galilee, but there was <u>no</u> <u>storm</u> now. There was no thunder or lightning, only the sound <u>as of</u> a rushing mighty wind coming down from <u>Heaven</u> and it <u>filled the house</u> where they were sitting.

I KINGS 8
Verse 10
And it came to pass, when the priests were come out of the holy place, that the cloud filled the house of the Lord.

We read the cloud in the Old Testament was the sign of Jehovah. It filled the house after the sacrifices were brought and offered to God when Solomon's temple was dedicated. But now Pentecost was a much greater event than the dedication of the temple.

I CORINTHIANS 6
Verse 19
What? Know ye not that your body is the temple of the Holy Ghost which is in you, which ye have of God, and ye are not your own?

2 CORINTHIANS 6
Verse 16
And what agreement hath the temple of God with idols? For ye are the temple of the living God; as God hath said, I will dwell in them, and walk in them; and I will be their God, and they shall be my people.
The house where the one hundred and twenty believers were assembled was filled with the <u>sound</u> from Heaven thus signifying that a much greater and nobler building (or temple) was about to be fulfilled on Earth as the habitation of God (or <u>a place to dwell in</u>).

ACTS 2
Verse 3
And there appeared unto them cloven tongues like as a fire, and it sat upon each of them.

ROMANS 10
Verse 17
So, then faith cometh by hearing, and hearing by the word of God.

Notice, the disciples heard the sound <u>as of</u> a mighty rushing <u>wind</u> even though the wind did not speak. The wind to them was a symbol of the Holy Spirit and the Holy Spirit must accompany the <u>word</u> or there can be no <u>living faith.</u> They first heard the sound then came the visible evidence of the coming of the Holy Spirit.

ACTS 2
Verse 4
And they were <u>all filled</u> with the Holy Ghost, and began to speak with other tongues, <u>as the Spirit gave them utterance.</u>

There appeared unto them cloven (or divided) tongues. Here cloven means "divided or parted". The tongues were separate one from the other and sat upon each of them (or on each individual). The Holy Ghost is not just a power, but He is a gift of God to all who believe.

The cloven (or parted) tongues were symbols of the diverse languages in which the believers would declare the grace of God to all people. The tongues were <u>like a fire</u> thus symbolic of <u>righteousness, holiness and judgment of Almighty God.</u>

DEUTERONOMY 4
Verse 24
For the Lord, thy God is a consuming fire, even a jealous God.

HEBREWS 12
Verse 29
For our God is a consuming fire.

Even though the tongues were not literal fire, they were visible, first filling the room and then coming to rest upon each of them. In the upper room, the tongues as of fire resembled the human tongue and now this miracle put a new tongue (and a new language) into the mouth of every person present. They spoke words they had never spoken before.

Let's notice one other time God's presence appeared in a <u>fire...</u>

EXODUS 19
Verse 18
And mount Sinai was altogether on a smoke, because the LORD descended upon it in fire: and the smoke thereof ascended as the smoke of a furnace, and the whole mount quaked greatly.

Notice, Moses had brought the people out to meet with God, and they stood at the <u>nether</u> (or the lowermost parts) of the mount.

ACTS 2
Verse 4
And they were <u>all filled</u> with the Holy Ghost, and began to speak with other tongues, <u>as the Spirit gave them utterance.</u>

Verse 5
And there were dwelling at Jerusalem Jews, <u>devout men</u>, out of every nation under heaven.

Verse 6
Now when this was noised abroad, the multitude came together, and were confounded (*or confused*), because that every man heard them speak in his own language.

GENESIS
Verse 1
And the whole earth was of one language, and of one speech.

Verse 7
Go to (*or come*), let us go down, and there confound their language, that they may not understand one another's speech.

Verse 8
So, the LORD scattered them abroad from thence upon the face of all the earth: and they left off to build the city.

Verse 9
Therefore, is the name of it called Babel; because the LORD did there confound the language of all the earth: and from thence did the LORD scatter them abroad upon the face of all the earth.

Notice, at the Tower of Babel the language was confounded (or confused) and the people were scattered over the face of the earth.
Now, here we see (in Acts) the nations coming together once more, this time hearing every man in his own language.
Notice how God first scattered them, and here they come together. This was the first time the Blessed Promise of the Holy Spirit was fulfilled.

The gift of tongues was the sign of the keeping of God's promise to send the Holy Spirit and a sign to the multitude gathered there.

Now let's go back…

ACTS 1
Verse 8 [a]
But ye shall receive power, after that the Holy Ghost is come upon you: and ye shall be witnesses unto me

The Spirit's ministry in the believer…
1. Regenerates; makes spiritually alive (John 3:5)
2. He indwells (I Corinthians 3:16)
3. Grants assurance (Romans 8:16)
4. Sanctifies or achieves holiness (I Corinthians 1:30)
5. Empowers spiritually (Acts 1:8 & Luke 10:10)
6. Leads and guides (Romans 8:14 & Galatians 5:25)
7. Assists in worship and prayer (John 16:14 & Ephesians 6:18)
8. Implements adoption (Romans 8:15-16)
9. Communes and fellowships (Philippians 2:11 & II Corinthians 13:14)

10. He anoints (I John 2:20-27)
    a. He abides
    b. He assures spiritual knowledge
    c. Conveys teaching
    d. Imparts truth
    e. Relates to abiding in Christ
11. He seals (Ephesians 1:13 & II Corinthians 1:22)
12. He teaches and reminds (John 14:16 & John 16:13)
13. He helps our infirmities (Romans 8:26)
14. He searches and makes intercession (Romans 8:27)

(Why Tongues?)

<u>As a sign</u>

JAMES 2
Verse 5
Even <u>so the tongue</u> is a little member, and boasteth great things. Behold, how great a matter a <u>little fire</u> kindleth!

Verse 6
And <u>the tongue</u> is a fire, a world of iniquity: so is the tongue among our members, that it defileth the whole body, and setteth on fire the course of nature; and it is set on fire of hell.

Verse 8
But the tongue can <u>no man</u> tame; it is an unruly evil, full of deadly poison.

PROVERBS 18
Verse 21
Death and life are in the power of the tongue: and they that love it shall eat the fruit thereof.

ACTS 2
Verse 33
Therefore, <u>being by</u> the right hand of God exalted, and <u>having received</u> of the Father the promise of the Holy Ghost, <u>he hath shed forth this</u>, which ye now <u>see</u> and <u>hear</u>.

This is why the Holy Spirit evidence comes by tongues because no man is able to tame it. We must yield it unto the Holy Spirit. In order for the Holy Spirit to work, man must surrender every part of his body.

ROMANS 6
Verse 11
Likewise, recon ye also yourselves to be dead indeed <u>unto sin</u>, <u>but alive unto God</u> through Jesus Christ our Lord.

Verse 12
Let not sin therefore reign in your <u>mortal</u> body, that ye should obey <u>it</u> in the lusts thereof.

Verse 13

Neither yield ye your members as instruments of unrighteousness unto sin: but yield yourselves unto God, as those that are alive from the dead, and your members as instruments of righteousness unto God.

We could go on and on about the Holy Ghost and its work in the believer. The tongue is the member of the body that man has the worst trouble with. It has the power of life and death in it. So, yield it to Christ.

CHAPTER 17
JESUS, THE GREAT INTERSSOR

> *JOHN 17*
> *Verse 20*
> *Neither pray I for these alone, but for them also which shall believe on me through their word;*

Intercession – meaning "an advocate" ("prayer offered on behalf of others")

I JOHN 2
Verse 1

My little children, these things write I unto you, that ye sin not. And if any man sin, we have an advocate with the Father, Jesus Christ the righteous:

There are three things Christ does for the believer...
1. He is a helper (John 14:26)
2. Suffered once just for unjust (I Peter 3:18)
3. The atoning sacrifice (Hebrews 2:17-18)

ROMANS 8
Verse 34

Who is he that condemneth? It is Christ that died, yea rather, that is risen again, who is even at the right hand of God, who also maketh intercession for us.

Here we see four redemptive acts of Jesus Christ...
1. His death
2. His resurrection
3. His ascension
4. His intercession

ROMANS 8
Verse 26

Likewise, the Spirit also helpeth our infirmities: for we know not what we should pray for as we ought: but the Spirit itself maketh intercession for us with groanings which cannot be uttered.

The word "helpeth" ...it is the assistance afforded by any two persons to each other who bear the same burden or carry t between them.

Verse 27

And he that searcheth the hearts knoweth what is the mind of the Spirit, because he maketh intercession for the saints according to the will of God.

Intercessor means "one who intercedes or acts as an agent or manager in all phases of salvation and dealings with God.

Let's notice Jesus' prayer in this chapter…

JOHN 17
Verse 13
And now come I to thee; and these things I speak in the world, <u>that</u> they might have my joy fulfilled in themselves.

Verse 14
I <u>have</u> given them thy word; and the world hath hated them, <u>because</u> they are not of the world, <u>even as</u> I am not of the world.

Verse 15
I pray not that thou shouldest take them out of the world, but that thou shouldest keep them from the evil.

He does not pray for them to die or leave this world but to live and be a light and an example of God in the world.

MATTHEW 5
Verse 16
Let your light so shine before men, that they may see your good works, and glorify your Father which is in heaven.

In Matthew 5 verse 13, Jesus says, "Ye are the salt of the earth. Salt means "a compound that gives flavor". In verses 14-16, He says, Ye are the light of the world. Light means "that which makes vision possible or brightness."

PHILIPPIANS 2
Verse 14
Do all things without murmurings and disputing.

Verse 15
Let your light so shine before men, that they may see your good works, and glorify your Father which is in heaven.

The proper place to let your light shine is among the <u>lost</u>, for in such a position can a true Christian witness…be an influence for the <u>gospel</u>. A true believer must be without rebuke (or fault) and they suffer no moral damage by acting like the world. They are to be a light to a dark world and be salt with much flavor. The stars only show when it is dark. So, let your light shine.

Verse 16
They are not of the world, <u>even as</u> I am not of the world.

Verse 17
<u>Sanctify them</u> through thy truth; they word is truth.

They were to separate from the world to a sacred use, to consecrate self wholly to God and His service. It means the person who is sanctified needs to be <u>separated</u> from sin and defilement in order to be fit to be used of God.

JOHN 17
Verse 19
And for their sakes I sanctify myself, <u>that</u> they also might be sanctified through the truth.

Notice, I separate myself unto God to do His will even unto death so that the believers may benefit through <u>me</u> (or Jesus Christ) for them and be sanctified continually as they get to know the word.

I JOHN 1
Verse 7
But if we walk in the light, as he is in the light, we have fellowship one with another, and <u>the blood</u> of Jesus Christ his Son cleanseth us from all sin.

Verse 20
Neither pray I for these alone, but for them also which shall believe in me through their word.

JOHN 10
Verse 16

And <u>other sheep</u> I have, which are not of this fold: them also I must bring, and they shall hear my voice; and there shall be <u>one-fold</u>, *and* <u>one shepherd</u>.

Verse 21

<u>That</u> they all <u>may be</u> one; as thou, Father, art in me, and I in thee, <u>that</u> they also may <u>be one in us</u>: that the world may believe that thou hast sent me.

Verse 23

I in them, and thou in me, <u>that</u> they may <u>be made perfect in one</u>; and that the world may know that thou hast sent me, and hast loved them, as thou hast loved me.

Verse 24

Father, I will that they also, whom <u>thou hast given me</u>, be with me where I am; that they may behold my glory, which <u>thou hast given me</u>: for thou lovedst me <u>before</u> the foundation of the world.

In this <u>great</u> chapter, we see ten times Jesus state "<u>I have</u>"

1. I have glorified them on earth (verse 4)
2. I have finished the work (verse 4)
3. I have manifested thy name (verse 6)
4. I have given them thy word (verse 8)
5. I have kept them (verse 12)
6. I have given them thy word (verse 14)
7. I have sent them into the world as you sent me (Verse 18)
8. I have given them thy glory (verse 22)
9. I have known thee (verse 25)
10. I have declared unto them thy name (verse 26)

What a wonderful intercessor and an advocate! Praise God for what this chapter means to the believer!

AMEN

> JOHN 18
> Verse 11
> *Then said Jesus unto Peter, Put up thy sword into the sheath: the cup which my Father hath given me, shall I not drink it?*

There are 12 cups in scripture...
1. Cup of judgment on the wicked (Psalms 11:6)
2. Cup of salvation and blessing (Psalms 16:5 & 116:13)
3. Cup of God's wrath (Isaiah 51:17-22 & Revelation 16:19)
4. Cup of consolation (Jeremiah 16:7)
5. Cup of chastening on the nations by Babylon (Jeremiah 51:7 & Revelation 18:6)
6. Cup of chastening on Israel by Gentiles (Lamentations 4:21 & Ezekiel 23:31-33)
7. Cup of filth and hypocrisy (Matthew 23:25-26)
8. Cup of sufferings of Christ (Matthew 20:22 & Mark 20:38)
9. Cup of death (Matthew 26:39-42 & Mark 14:36)
10. Cup of the last supper (Matthew 26:27-28, I Corinthians 10:16-21 & I Corinthians 11:25)
11. Cup of communion with Satan (I Corinthians 10:21)
12. Cup of abominations (Revelation 17:4)

MATTHEW 20
Verse 22
But Jesus answered and said, <u>ye know not</u> what ye ask. Are ye able to drink of the cup that I shall drink of, and to be baptized with the baptism that I am baptized with? They say unto him, we are able.

They could drink of the cup. He said, "Ye shall drink indeed." But the cup of suffering was yet to be fulfilled.

LUKE 22
Verse 42
Saying, Father, if thou be willing, remove this cup from me: nevertheless, not my will, but thine, be done.

Verse 44
And being in an agony he prayed more earnestly: and his sweat was as it were great drops of blood falling down to the ground.

This proves that Christ was in a <u>life and death</u> struggle in the garden and He was not going through an ordinary prayer, because of the sweat becoming great <u>drops of blood.</u> He was about to face sin and death for us

I PETER 2
Verse 24
Who his own self bare our sins in his own body on the tree that we, being dead to sins, should live unto righteousness: by whose stripes ye were healed.

I PETER 3
Verse 18

For Christ, also hath once suffered for sins, the just for the unjust, that he might bring us to God, being put to death in the flesh, but quickened by the Spirit:

There are four things Christ did:
1. He suffered as our example (1 Peter 2:21)
2. He was committed to God's cause (1 Peter 2:23)
3. He bore our sins in His own body (I Peter 2:24)
4. He submitted to stripes to heal us (I Peter 2:24 & Isaiah 53:4-6)

Also note three reasons for His death:
1. That we might be dead to sin (Romans 6:6-7)
2. That we might live to righteousness (Romans 3:26)
3. That we might be healed (Isaiah 53:4-6 & I Peter 2:24)

Now let's note...

I PETER 3
Verse 18

For Christ, also hath once suffered for sins, the just for the unjust, that he might bring us to God, being put to death in the flesh, but quickened by the Spirit:

There are three purposes of Christ's suffering:
1. He suffered for sin (Galatians 1:4)
2. He suffered for the injust (Romans 5:6-8)
3. He suffered to bring us to God (Colossians 2:14-17 & I Peter 3:18)

In verse 18 He was put to death in the flesh. Notice, He died in the flesh only. <u>He did not die in the spirit</u> proving immortality of the spirit.

JAMES 2
Verse 26

For as the body without the spirit is dead, so faith without works is dead also.

Let's notice once again the question of Jesus..." Are ye able to drink of the cup?" The cup in which He drank was for all mankind. He became sin for us. He who knew no sin that we might become the righteousness of God.

2 CORINTHIANS 5
Verse 21

For he hath made him to be sin for us, who knew no sin; that we might be made the righteousness of God in him.

This wonderful chapter explains just a few of the lonely cups that Jesus had to drink in order that we could become the righteousness of God.

Thank God
Amen

CHAPTER 19
JESUS, THE UPLIFTED SAVIOR

JOHN 19

Verse 16

Then delivered he him therefore unto them to be crucified. And they took Jesus, and led him away.

Verse 17

And he bearing his cross went forth into a place called the place of a skull, which is called in the Hebrew Golgotha:

Verse 18

Where they crucified him, and two other with him, on either side one, and Jesus in the midst.

JOHN 3
Verse 14
And as Moses lifted up the serpent in the wilderness, even so must the Son of man be lifted up:

MATTHEW 27
Verse 26
Then released he Barabbas unto them: and when he had scourged Jesus, he delivered him to be crucified.

Verse 27
Then the soldiers of the governor took Jesus into the common hall, and gathered unto him the whole band of soldiers.

Verse 28
And they stripped him, and put on him a scarlet robe.

Verse 29
And when they had platted a crown of thorns, they put it upon his head, and a reed in his right hand: and they bowed the knee before him, and mocked him, saying, Hail, King of the Jews!

There are several scriptures we want to look at concerning His crucifixion.

They stripped him...

LUKE 23
Verse 11
And Herod with his men of war set him at nought, and mocked him, and arrayed him in a gorgeous robe, and sent him again to Pilate.

ACTS 4
Verse 26
The kings of the earth stood up (*or took their stand*), and the rulers were gathered together against the Lord, and against his Christ.

Verse 27
For of a truth against thy holy child Jesus (*or servant*), whom thou hast anointed, both Herod, and Pontius Pilate, with the Gentiles, and the people of Israel, were gathered together,

Verse 28
For to do whatsoever thy hand and thy counsel (*or purpose*) determined before to be done.

Here in Verse 27 we see them taking a stand against Christ whom God had predetermined Jesus to save the lost humanity. Jesus came to bring it to pass.

God determined two things...
1. To give up His Son to die or sinners (Romans 5:8)
2. To give sinners their own free will so that while they resisted His will they would fulfill it by crucifying the only one who was destined to save all who believed (John 3:16)

Let's go back to Matthew

MATTHEW 27
Verse 29
And when they had platted (*or twisted*) a crown of thorns, they put it upon his head, and a reed in his right hand: and they bowed the knee before him, and mocked him, saying, Hail, King of the Jews!

Verse 30
And they spit upon him, and took the reed, and smote him on the head.

Verse 31
And after that they had mocked him, they took the robe off from him, and put his own raiment on him, and led him away to crucify him.

Now carefully watch this...

PSALMS 22
Verse 1
My God, my God, why hast thou forsaken me? Why art thou so far from helping me, and from the words of my roaring (*or groaning*)?"

Psalms 22
Verse 6
But I am a worm, and no man; a reproach of men, and despised of the people.

PSALMS 109
Verse 6
<u>I became</u> a reproach unto them: when they looked upon me they shaked their heads.

"I am a reproach" meaning I am the lowest of the people and no great man.

The word "worm" meaning he took the lowest form among men to be rejected, or to be refused or disowned.

The word "scorned" meaning he took the cruelty of beating at the judgment hall, thirty-nine stripes.

The words "spit upon" meaning to eject from the mouth. It was considered uncleanness as in the cleansing of a disease in the Old Testament, called a copulation. (Copulation meaning sexual disease – Strong's #7901 Shakab.

LEVITICUS 15
Verse 1
And the LORD Spake unto Moses and to Aaron, saying,

Verse 2
Speak unto the children of Israel, and say unto them, When any man hath a running issue out of his flesh, because of his issue he is unclean.

Verse 3
And this shall be his uncleanness in his issue: whether his flesh run with his issue, or his flesh be stopped from his issue, it is his uncleanness.

Verse 4
Every bed, whereon he lieth that hath the issue, is unclean: and everything, whereon he sitteth, shall be unclean.

Verse 5
And whosoever toucheth his bed shall wash his clothes, and bathe himself in water, and be unclean until the even.

Verse 6
And he that sitteth on any thing whereon he sat that hath the issue shall wash his clothes, and bathe himself in water, and be unclean until the even.

Verse 7
And he that toucheth the flesh of him that hath the issue shall wash his clothes, and bathe himself in water, and be unclean until the even.

Verse 8
And if he that hath the issue spit upon him that is clean; then he shall wash his clothes, and bathe himself in water, and be unclean until the even

Verse 15
And the priest shall offer them, the one for a sin offering, and the other for a burnt offering; and the priest shall make an atonement for him before the Lord for his issue.

PSALMS 22
Verse 7
All they that see me laugh me to scorn: they shoot out the lip (*or show contempt with their mouth*), they shake the head, saying,

Verse 8
He trusted on the Lord that he would deliver him: let him deliver him, seeing he delighted in him.

Let's look at this entire chapter (Psalms 22) ...there are thirty facts and sufferings of our precious Lord.

1. I am forsaken by God (Verse 1)
2. I am far from being helped (Verse 1)
3. I am far from being heard (Verse 1)
4. I am a worm (Verse 6)
5. I am a reproach of men (Verse 6)
6. I am despised of the people (Verse 6)
7. I am no man (Verse 6)
8. I am scorned by men (Verse 7)
9. I am mocked by men (Verses 7 & 8)
10. God is my protector from birth (Verses 7 & 8)
11. God is my hope from birth (Verse 9)
12. God is my dependence from birth (Verse 9-12)
13. Jehovah is my God from birth (Verse 10)
14. God has always been near me (Verse 11)
15. I have had to face trouble (Verse 11)
16. God has been my only help (Verse 11)
17. Brutal men have compassed me (Verse 12)
18. Men were determined to destroy me (Verse 13)
19. My life blood is poured out like water (Verse 14)
20. All my bones are out of joint (Verse 14)
21. My heart is melted like wax in the midst of my bowels (Verse 14)
22. My strength is gone (Verse 15)
23. My tongue is so dry it cleaves to my jaws (Verse 15)
24. I am slain as a sacrifice (Verse 15)
25. Gentiles have compassed me (Verse 16)
26. The wicked enclose me (Verse 16)
27. My hands and feet are pierced (Verse 16)
28. My bones are out of joint and men stare at me (Verse 17)
29. My garments are coveted (Verse 18)
30. Men gamble for my vesture (Verse 18)

I PETER 2
Verse 24
Who his own self bare our sins <u>in his own body</u> on the tree that we, being dead to sins, should live unto righteousness: <u>by</u> whose stripes ye were healed.

ISAIAH 53
Verse 1
Who hath believed our report? And to whom is the arm of the LORD revealed?

Verse 2
For he shall grow up before him as a tender plant, and as a root out of a dry ground: he hath no form nor comeliness; and when we shall see him, there is no beauty that we should desire him.

Verse 3
He is despised and rejected of men; a man of sorrows, and acquainted with grief: and we hid as it were our faces from him; he was despised, and we esteemed him not.

Verse 4
Surely he hath borne our griefs, and carried our sorrows: yet we did esteem him stricken, smitten of God, and afflicted.

Verse 5
But he was wounded for our transgressions, he was bruised for our iniquities: the chastisement of our peace was upon him; and with his stripes we are healed.

Verse 6
All we like sheep have gone astray; we have turned everyone to his own way; and the Lord hath laid on him the iniquity of us all.

Verse 7
He was oppressed, and he was afflicted, yet he opened not his mouth: he is brought as a lamb to the slaughter, and as a sheep before her shearers is dumb, so he openeth not his mouth.

Verse 8
He was taken from prison and from judgment: and who shall declare his generation? For he was cut off out of the land of the living: for the transgression of my people was he stricken.

Verse 9
And he made his grave with the wicked, and with the rich in his death; because he had don no violence, neither was any deceit in his mouth.

PSALMS 129
Verse 3
The plowers plowed upon my back: they made long their furrows.

COLOSSIANS 2
Verse 13
And you, being dead in your sins and the uncircumcision of your flesh, hath he <u>quickened together with him, having forgiven you all</u> trespasses;

Verse 14
<u>Blotting out the handwriting</u> of ordinances that was against us, which was contrary to us, <u>and took it out of the way</u>, nailing it to his cross;

Verse 15
<u>And having spoiled</u> principalities and powers, he <u>made a shew of them openly, triumphing over them</u> in it.

He, blotted out the handwriting against us; therefore, it can be <u>seen no more (or for ever more)</u>. This handwriting was usually a decree, but here it represents the <u>Law of Moses.</u>

<u>Taking it out of the way</u>...The Law of Moses was against us as only the blood of <u>bulls and goats</u> were offered for sins. But here, Christ took it out of the way by his own sacrifice or <u>redemption</u> could never be experienced. The Law made no provisions for <u>redemption</u>. It only cursed and killed men who broke the Law. He took it out of the way by nailing it to His cross.

Note Moses' law was annulled. This is simply how He took the Law of Moses out of the way. He nailed it to His cross and annulled its penalty so we could have a new start in life before God (<u>or being born again</u>). He crucified the thing that brought guilt and death to all men.

Notice Verse 15
1. Abolished and cancelled the law by
   a. Blotting it out (Verse 14)
   b. Taking it out of the way (Verse 14)
   c. By nailing it to His cross

2. By defeating the executors of the Law by
   a. Sporting of conquering them (Verse 15)
   b. By making a show of them openly (Verse 15)
   c. Triumphing over them in the very crops that they thought was a triumph over Him (Verse 15)

"Spoiled principalities and powers" means to strip off the clothes of another and to put off. Here it means Satan and his forces were stripped of their power to condemn and kill the human race. The Law was blotted out and could no longer hold men in sin and bondage. Jesus set us free.

COLOSSIANS 3
Verse 8
<u>But now</u> ye also <u>put off</u> all these; anger, wrath, malice, blasphemy, filthy communication out of your mouth.

Verse 9
<u>Lie not</u> one to another, seeing that ye have <u>put off the old man</u> with his deeds;

There are two kinds of old things that pass away (or put off).

1. The spirit nature and power of sin working in men to disobedience (Ephesians 2:2)

John 19
Verse 17
And he bearing his cross went forth into a place called the place of a skull, which is called in the <u>Hebrew Golgotha</u>:

Verse 18
Where they crucified him, and two other with him, on either side one, and Jesus in the midst.

Verse 28
After this, Jesus knowing that all things were now accomplished, that the scripture might be fulfilled, saith, <u>I thirst</u>.

2. Outward sin or transgression of the Law (Romans 6:6 and 1 John 3:4)

<u>I Thirst</u>

JOHN 4
Verse 13
Jesus answered and said unto her, whosoever drinketh of this water shall thirst again:

Verse 14
But whosoever drinketh of the water that I shall give him shall never thirst; but the water that I shall give him shall be in him a well of water springing up into everlasting life.

GENESIS 1
Verse 9
And God said, let the waters under the heaven be gathered together unto one place, and let the dry land appear: and it was so.

JOB 26
Verse 12
He divideth the sea with his power, and by his understanding he smiteth through the proud.

He spoke and seas came in to view (or being). He speaks and divideth the Red Sea and by his understanding he stirreth up and smiteth through the storms. Now we have the very one who said let there be and it was so now the one who is the water of life says, "<u>I thirst</u>".

PSALMS 22
Verse 15
My strength is dried up like a potsherd (*or a piece of broken pottery*); and my tongue cleaveth to my jaws; and thou hast brought me into the dust of death.

Here Christ was brought down to death and His body was like that of Adam <u>before God breathed into him.</u> He was now showing the God man that He must die in the stead of man for their sins.

John 19
Verse 30
When Jesus therefore had received the vinegar, he said<u>, it is finished</u>: and he bowed his head, and gave up the ghost.

What is finished?

1. Fulfillment of all scriptures about sufferings (Isaiah 53)
2. Defeat of Satan (John 12:31-32)
3. Breaking down the middle wall to make Jews and Gentiles <u>one</u> (I Corinthians 12:13-14)
4. Personal access to God (Ephesians 2:18)
5. Cancellation of the reign of <u>death</u> (Romans 5:12-21)
6. Cancellation of sin's power (Romans 6:1-23)
7. Obedient unto death (Philippians 2:8)
8. Perfection of Christ (Hebrews 2:10 & 5:8-11)
9. Salvation from all sin (Colossians 1:14)
10. Making peace between God and man (Colossians 1:20-22)
11. Death penalty paid for all (Hebrews 2:9-15 & I Peter 1:19)
12. Cancellation of the claims Satan had and freeing man from his sin (Colossians 2:13-15)
13. Satisfaction of justice of God (Genesis 2:17 & John 3:16)
14. Bodily healing for us (Isaiah 53:4-5 & I Peter 2:14)
15. Enduement of power and anointing of the Holy Spirit (John 7:38-39 & Acts 1:4-8)
16. Blotting out of the old convenant and making and sealing of the new (Colossians 2:14-17 & Hebrews 7:11-28)

<u>Thank God it is finished!</u>

John 19
Verse 34
But one of the soldiers with a <u>spear pierced his side</u>, and forthwith came there out blood and water.

GENESIS 2
Verse 21
And the LORD God caused a deep sleep to fall upon Adam, and he slept: and he took one of his ribs, and closed up the flesh instead thereof;

As Adam's side was opened up to take a rib to make his bride. Now we see if Adam's side must be opened to bring forth a bride, Christ's side must also be opened in order to receive His bride in whom He gave His life for her. Wherefore, came forth blood and water, signifying thus we must be born of water and of Spirit. (John 3:5)

Water represents being born by the Word (John 15:3 & James 1:18 & Ephesians 5:26)

Spirit represents a well of living water (John 7:37-39 & Romans 8:9)

JOHN 19
Verse 41
Now in the place where he was crucified there was a garden; and in the garden a new sepulchre, wherein was never man yet laid.

Verse 42
There laid they Jesus therefore because of the Jews' preparation day; for the sepulchre was nigh at hand.

MATTHEW 27
Verse 59
And when Joseph had taken the body, he wrapped it in a clean linen cloth,

Verse 60
And laid it in his own new tomb, which he had hewn out in the rock: and he rolled a great stone to the door of the sepulchre, and departed.

Thank God! They may have buried Him, but the grave could not hold Him! Praise God for this great chapter!

CHAPTER 20
JESUS, THE CONQUEROR OF DEATH

JOHN 20
Verse 1
The first day of the week cometh Mary Magdalene early, when it was yet dark, unto the sepulchre, and seeth the stone taken away from the sepulchre.

MATTHEW 28
Verse 6
He is not here: for he is risen, as he said. Come, see the place where the Lord lay.

LUKE 24
Verse 3
And they entered in, and found not the body of the Lord Jesus

The Empty Tomb

LUKE 24
Verse 12
<u>Then arose Peter</u>, and ran unto the sepulchre; and stooping down, he beheld the linen clothes laid by themselves, and departed, wondering in himself at that which was come to pass.

There are six things Peter did in this verse:

1. Arose
2. Ran
3. Stooped
4. Saw
5. Departed
6. Wondered

These six things he did, but the most important thing he didn't do in all of this was one word...<u>believe.</u> But it did not occur to him to believe even when he saw the linen clothes. He laid them by themselves when he arose.

JOHN 20
Verse 6
Then cometh Simon Peter following him, and went into the sepulchre, and seeth the linen clothes lie,

Verse 7
And the napkin, that was about his head, not lying with the linen clothes, but wrapped together in a place by itself.

Notice, these things or linen clothes that were wrapped about Him were lying in place as though He had just slipped out of them. But the napkin was placed in a separate place by itself. He merely passed out of them not <u>needing someone</u> to lose Him and let Him go as in the story of Lazarus.

JOHN 11
Verse 44
And <u>he that was dead came forth</u>, bound hand and foot with grave clothes: and his face was bound about with a napkin. <u>Jesus saith</u> unto them, loose him, and let him go.

Lazarus had to be loosed and let go. But the clothes that Jesus left behind was proof that <u>He</u> had risen and left them behind.

So, we don't leave anything uncovered about <u>His resurrection </u>(bodily resurrection, as His <u>spirit </u>and <u>soul</u> <u>never</u> <u>died</u>, only His <u>body</u>), let's look at several proofs of His bodily resurrection...

"Resurrection" meaning the act of rising from the dead. Let's look then at...

1. My hands and feet (Luke 24:39)
2. It's I, not another person or different (Luke 24:39)
3. Handle me and see (Luke 24:39)
4. A spirit hath not flesh and bone (Luke 24:39)
5. He showed them His hand and feet (Luke 24:40)
6. He took fish and honeycomb and did eat before them (Luke 24:41-43)
7. He is risen (Matthew 28:6-7 & Mark 16:6)
   a. What is risen? It could not have been His spirit and soul for they went and preached to the spirits in prison.
      - I Peter 3: 19: By which also he went and preached unto the spirits in prison
      - Hebrews 2:14: Forasmuch then as the children are partakers of flesh and blood, he also himself likewise took (*or shared*) part of the same; that through death he might destroy him that had the power of death, that is, the devil;
   b. His body is the only thing that died (James 2:26a), and the only thing that could have been resurrected was his body (Luke 24:39 & Zechariah 13:6)
8. They held him by His feet (Luke 24:39-40)
9. They saw Him (John 20:12-20 & Matthew 28:1)
10. They found not the body at the empty tomb (Luke 24:3)
11. Why seek ye the living among the dead (*bodies*) (Luke 24:5-6)
    a. Did they go to the tomb to perfume it with spices seeking a spirit to embalm or was it a body they sought? It was the body that was resurrected from the dead.
12. Jesus Himself drew near and sat a meat with them and they knew Him (Luke 24:15 & Luke 24:30-31)
13. Angels said He was alive (Luke 24:24; Matthew 28:6-7 & Mark 16:6)
14. Jesus Himself stood in the midst of them (Luke 24:37)
    a. They thought He was a spirit. Jesus assured them that it was His own body (Luke 24:39-34)
15. It behoved Him to be crucified and to be raised from the dead (Luke 24:46
16. He lifted up His hands and was parted from them and carried into Heaven (Luke 24:50-52 & Acts 1:11)
17. They have taken away our Lord from the sepulcher for as yet they <u>knew not</u> the scripture that He must be raised from the dead (John 20:2-9)
    a. It was resurrected and is alive today at the right hand of God (Acts 2:33; Romans 8:34; Hebrews 1:8 & 12:2)
18. (Thomas) Except I shall see his hands and the print of nails and thrust my hand in his side <u>I will not believe</u>. (John 20:25-29)
19. In the resurrection, the scriptures says it was raised (Acts 2:31; Acts 4:33 & I Peter 3:21)
20. One shall say, "And one shall say unto him, what are these wounds in thine hands? Then he shall answer, those with which I was wounded in the house of my friends." (Zechariah 13:6)
21. He was buried but He rose again (I Corinthians 15:1-58)

Thank God, He was crucified and buried and He rose again and went to the Father to be an advocate for us. (I John 2:1)

Praise God for this chapter!

CHAPTER 21
JESUS, THE RESTORER OF PENITENCE

Penitence – Meaning sorrow for one's <u>shortcomings</u>.

JOHN 21
Verse 15

So, when they had dined, Jesus saith to Simon Peter, Simon, son of Jonas, <u>lovest thou me more than these?</u> He saith unto him, Yea, Lord; thou knowest that I love thee. He saith unto him, Feed my lambs.

Verse 16

He saith to him again the second time, Simon, son of Jonas, lovest thou me? He saith unto him, Yea, Lord; thou knowest that <u>I love thee</u>. He saith unto him, <u>Feed my sheep</u>.

Verse 17

He saith unto him <u>the third time</u>, Simon, son of Jonas, lovest thou me? Peter was grieved because he said unto him the third time, Lovest thou me? And he said unto him, Lord, <u>thou knowest all things</u>; thou knowest that I love thee. Jesus saith unto him, <u>Feed my sheep</u>.

Peter had been told by Jesus that before the cock crows "thou shalt deny me thrice."

LUKE 22
Verse 34

And he said, I tell thee, Peter, the cock shall not crow this day, before that thou shalt thrice deny that thou knowest me.

MATTHEW 26
Verse 31

Then saith Jesus unto them, all ye shall be <u>offended</u> because of me this night: <u>for it is written</u>, I will smite the shepherd, and the sheep of the flock shall be scattered abroad.

Verse 32

But when I am risen again, I will go before you into Galilee.

Verse 33

Peter answered and said unto him, though all men shall be offended because of thee, yet will I never be offended.

Verse 34

Jesus said unto him, Verily I say unto thee, that <u>this night</u>, before the cock crow, thou shalt deny me thrice.

Verse 35

Peter said unto him, though I should die with thee, <u>yet will I not</u> deny thee. Likewise, also said all the disciples.

Peter denied Jesus three times. Now in John 21, Jesus is confronting him three times..." Lovest thou me more than these?" Notice, Peter bragged that he would not be offended and he was ready to die with Him.

1. <u>Deny</u> once (Matthew 26:69-70)
2. <u>Deny</u> twice (Matthew 26:71-72)
3. <u>Deny</u> thrice (Matthew 26:73-75)

Let's notice what Jesus said.

LUKE 22
Verse 31
And the Lord said, Simon, Simon, behold, Satan hath desired to have you, that he may sift you as wheat:

Verse 32
But I have prayed for thee, <u>that thy faith fail not</u>: and when thou art <u>converted</u>, strengthen thy brethren.

Satan obtained permission to tempt Job.

JOB 1
Verse 8
And the LORD said unto Satan, Hast thou considered my servant Job (*or have you set your heart on Job?*), that there is none like him in the earth, a perfect (*or blameless*) and an upright man, one that feareth God, and escheweth (*or shuns*) evil?

Verse 12
And the LORD said unto Satan, Behold, all that he hath is in thy power (*or thy hand*); only upon himself (*or his person*) put not forth thine hand. So, Satan went forth from the presence of the LORD.

Notice, God permits but does not order Satan to test Job. Satan's power is always <u>exercised under the control of God.</u> He is limited by the unlimited power of God. No doubt, now, Peter had begun to see what Jesus meant in Luke 22:31-32. God knew Peter would fall, for He stated in Verse 32 "I have prayed for thee, that thy faith fail not." He knew Peter would deny him and after his fall, he would have a repentant heart.

LUKE 22
Verse 62
And Peter went out, and wept bitterly.

For Jesus had said, "And when thou art <u>converted</u>, strengthen thy brethren.

This does not mean Peter had not been converted, for he had walked with Jesus now about three years. It simply means he was headed for a fall and that he would come back to God and after Pentecost he became much stronger than before.

Strengthen thy brothern

LUKE 22
Verse 31
And the Lord said, Simon, Simon, behold, Satan hath desired (*or Satan hath demanded to obtain by* asking) to have you, that he may sift you as wheat:

Verse 32
But I have prayed for thee (*evidently God grants permission*), that thy faith fail not: and when thou art converted (*or turned around again*), strengthen thy brethren.

PROVERBS 16
Verse 18
Pride goeth before destruction, and an haughty spirit before a fall (*or before a stumbling*).

UKE 22:33
And he said unto him, Lord, I am ready to go with thee, both into prison, and to death.

This pride was the downfall of Peter.

I CORINTHIANS 10
Verse 12
Wherefore let him that thinketh he standeth take heed lest he fall.

Peter made a brag about how much he loved Jesus. But notice, Peter once again opens his pride and it condemns him once again.

MARK 14
Verse 29
But Peter said unto him, although all shall be offended (*or caused to stumble*), yet will not I.

Verse 31
But he (*being Peter*) spake the more vehemently, If I should die with thee, I will not deny thee in any wise (*or never deny thee*). Likewise, also said they all.

JOHN 13
Verse 23
Now there was leaning on Jesus' bosom one of his disciples, whom Jesus loved.

JOHN 19
Verse 26
When Jesus therefore saw his mother, and the disciple standing by, whom he loved, he saith unto his mother, Woman, behold thy son!

Verse 27

Then saith he to the disciple, Behold thy mother! And from that hour that disciple took her unto his own home.

Now, let's notice…

JOHN 21
Verse 20
Then Peter, turning about, seeth the disciple <u>whom Jesus loved</u> following; which also leaned on his breast at supper, and said, Lord, which is he that betrayeth thee?

Verse 21
Peter seeing him saith to Jesus, Lord, and <u>what shall this man do</u>?

Verse 22
Jesus saith unto him, If I will that he tarry till I come, <u>what is that to thee? Follow thou</u> me.

Peter had his instructions:

1. Feed my lambs
2. Feed my sheep
3. Feed my sheep

Lambs

Peter is now instructed to be able to feed the lambs of the Gentile church.
JOHN 21
Verse 15

Now watch

JOHN 10
Verse 16
And other sheep I have, which are not of this fold: them also I must bring, and they shall hear my voice; and there shall be one-fold, and one shepherd.

Peter was instructed to feed by the lams and also the sheep

Sheep
JOHN 21
Verse 16

The house of Ephraim (<u>Jew and Gentile</u>)
The house of Mannasses (<u>or Israel</u>)

So, let's see what happens to Peter after Pentecost.

ACTS 10
Verse 13
And there came a voice to him, Rise, Peter; kill, and eat.

Verse 14
But Peter said, not so, Lord; for I have never eaten any thing that is common or unclean. **Verse 15**
And the voice spake unto him again the second time, what God hath cleansed, that call not thou common.

Verse 16
This was done thrice (*or three times*): and the vessel was received up again into heaven.

Peter once again made a statement about what God had cleansed at the cross by the rending (or tearing) the veil in twain (or in two) opening up the way for the Jew and Gentile.

1. Peter denied three times
2. Jesus asked Peter, "Lovest thou me?" three times
3. Peter sees the unclean, four-footed beasts three times and then three men seek him in Verse 19.

Since Jews and Gentiles were represented by the animal sacrifices, showing how God would also save the Gentiles, as the middle wall was now broken down, it was Peter's duty to preach to both the lams and also the sheep.

EPHESIANS 2
Verse 14
For he (*or himself*) is our peace, who hath made both one, and hath broken down the middle wall of partition (*or* division) between us;

Verse 15
Having abolished in his flesh the enmity (*or active mutual hatred*), even the law of commandments (*or to fulfill not to* destroy) contained in ordinances; for to make (*or create*) in himself of twain (*or the Jew and the Gentile*) one new man, so making peace;

The Law was meant to protect the Jews from pagan religion. By this, the Jews felt superior over the Gentiles. But Jesus abolished this hatred caused by the abuse of the law at Calvary by making the Law invalid to the church (of twain one new man), as Christian Jews and Christian Gentiles now compose this one new man or the Christian Church.

ACTS 10
Verse 27
And as he talked with him, he went in, and found many that were come together

Verse 28
And he said unto them, Ye know that it is an unlawful thing for a man that is a Jew to keep company, or come unto one of another nation; but God hath showed me that I should not call any man common or unclean.

Notice, Peter denied Christ three times. Jesus asked Peter, "Lovest thou me?" three times. Peter saw a vision of the Gentile three times. There were three Gentile men at the gate.

Let's look at Peter one more time. In Luke. It states, "When thou art converted..." Converted means to revert, to turn around (Strong's #1994 – Epistrepo). In other words, Jesus was telling Peter, "When you get turned around, you can feed my lambs and my sheep, bringing both Jew and Gentile together to be a Christian body.

Summary of the Gospel of John...in

Chapter 1 – he is THE SON OF GOD
Chapter 2 – he is THE SON OF MAN
Chapter 3 – he is THE DEVINE TEACHER
Chapter 4 – he is THE SOUL WINNER
Chapter 5 – he is THE GREAT PHYSICIAN
Chapter 6 – he is THE BREAD OF LIFE
Chapter 7 – he is THE WATER OF LIFE
Chapter 8 – he is THE DEFENDER OF THE WEAK
Chapter 9 – he is THE LIGHT OF THE WORLD
Chapter 10 – he is THE GOOD SHEPHERD
Chapter 11 – he is THE PRINCE OF LIFE
Chapter 12 – he is THE KING
Chapter 13 – he is THE SERVANT
Chapter 14 – he is THE COUNSELOR
Chapter 15 – he is THE TRUE VINE
Chapter 16 – he is THE GIVER OF THE HOLY SPIRIT
Chapter 17 – he is THE GREAT INTERCESSOR
Chapter 18 – he is THE SUFFERING SAVIOR
Chapter 19 – he is THE UPLIFTED SAVIOR
Chapter 20 – he is THE CONQUEROR OF DEATH
Chapter 21 – he is THE RESTORER OF THE PENITENCE

These are the great stories of Christ in the book of St. John

---

JOHN 21
Verse 25
And there are also many other things which Jesus did, the which, if they should be written everyone (or one by one) I suppose that even the world itself could not contain the books that should be written.

AMEN!

Let's worship Him for all He has given us!

Brother Carl
Copyright 2014

Printed in Great Britain
by Amazon

22216212R00064